MEASURING THE WORLD

Daniel Kehlmann

Translated from the German by
Carol Brown Janeway

ISIS
LARGE PRINT
Oxford

Copyright © Rowohlt Verlag GmbH,
Reinbek bei Hamburg, 2005
Translation Copyright © Carol Brown Janeway, 2006

First published in Great Britain 2007
by
Quercus

Published in Large Print 2008 by ISIS Publishing Ltd.,
7 Centremead, Osney Mead, Oxford OX2 0ES
by arrangement with
Quercus

British Library Cataloguing in Publication Data
Kehlmann, Daniel 1975–
    Measuring the world. – Large print ed.
    1. Humboldt, Alexander von, 1769–1859 – Fiction
    2. Gauss, Carl Friedrich, 1777–1855 – Fiction
    3. Biographical fiction
    4. Large type books
    I. Title
    833.9'14 [F]

ISBN 978–0–7531–8026–6 (hb)
ISBN 978–0–7531–8027–3 (pb)

Printed and bound in Great Britain by
T. J. International Ltd., Padstow, Cornwall

The Journey

In September 1828, the greatest mathematician in the country left his hometown for the first time in years, to attend the German Scientific Congress in Berlin. Naturally he had no desire to go. He had been declining to accept for months, but Alexander von Humboldt had remained adamant, until in a moment of weakness and the hope that the day would never come, he had said yes.

So now Professor Gauss was hiding in bed. When Minna told him he must get up, the coach was waiting and it was a long journey, he wrapped his arms around the pillow and tried to make his wife disappear by closing his eyes. When he opened them again and Minna was still there, he told her she was a hindrance, and limited, and the misfortune of his old age. When that didn't work either, he pushed back the coverlet and set his feet on the floor.

Bad-temperedly, he performed the most minimal ablutions and went downstairs. In the parlor, his son Eugen was waiting with a bag packed. As Gauss caught sight of him, he flew into a rage: he broke a jug that was standing on the windowsill, stamped his foot, and struck out wildly. He wasn't even to be calmed when Eugen to one side of him and Minna to the other laid their hands on his shoulders and swore that he would be well taken care of, he would soon be home again, and everything would be over in no time, just like a bad dream. Only when his ancient mother, disturbed by the noise, emerged from her room to pinch his cheek and ask what had happened to her brave boy did he pull himself together. Without warmth he said goodbye to Minna, and absent-mindedly stroked the heads of his daughter and youngest son. Then he allowed himself to be helped into the coach.

The journey was a torture. He called Eugen a failure, took the knobbed stick away from him, and jabbed it full force at his foot. For a time he stared out of the window, a frown on his face, then asked when his daughter was finally going to get married. Why didn't anyone want her, what was the problem?

Eugen pushed back his long hair, kneaded his red cap with both hands, and didn't want to answer.

Out with it, said Gauss.

To be honest, said Eugen, his sister wasn't exactly pretty.

Gauss nodded; the answer seemed a plausible one. He said he wanted a book.

Eugen gave him the one he had just opened: Friedrich Jahn's *German Gymnastics*. It was one of his favorites.

Gauss tried to read, but seconds later he was already glancing up to complain about the newfangled leather suspension on the coach; it made you feel even sicker than usual. Soon, he explained, machines would be carrying people from town to town at the speed of a shot. Then you'd do the trip from Göttingen to Berlin in half an hour.

Eugen shrugged.

It was both odd and unjust, said Gauss, a real example of the pitiful arbitrariness of existence, that you were born into a particular time and held prisoner there whether you wanted it or not. It gave you an indecent advantage over the past and made you a clown vis-à-vis the future.

Eugen nodded sleepily.

Even a mind like his own, said Gauss, would have been incapable of achieving anything in early human history or on the banks of the Orinoco, whereas in another two hundred years each and every idiot would be able to make fun of him and invent the most complete nonsense about his character. He thought things over, called Eugen a failure again, and turned his attention to the book. As he read, Eugen in his distress turned his face fixedly to the window, to hide his look of mortification and anger.

German Gymnastics was all about exercise equipment. The author expounded at length on this or that piece of apparatus which he had invented for swinging oneself up or around on. He called one the pommel horse, another the beam, and another the vaulting horse.

The man was out of his mind, said Gauss, opened the window, and threw the book out.

That was his book, cried Eugen.

Quite so, said Gauss, dropped off to sleep, and didn't stir until they reached the stop at the frontier that evening and the horses were being changed.

While the old horses were being unhitched and the new ones harnessed up, they ate potato soup in an inn. The only other guest, a thin man with a long beard and hollow cheeks, inspected them furtively from the next table. Everything pertaining to the body, said Gauss, who to his irritation had been dreaming about gym apparatus, was the true source of all humiliation. He had always considered it a sign of God's malicious sense of humor that a spirit such as his should be trapped in a sickly body while a common or garden-variety creature like Eugen was, to all intents and purposes, never ill.

He had had a severe attack of smallpox when he was a child, said Eugen. He had almost died. You could still see the scars!

True, said Gauss, he'd forgotten. He pointed to the post horses outside the window. It was actually quite funny that the rich needed twice as much time to make a journey as the poor. If you used post horses, you could change them after every section. If you had your own, you had to wait until they were fresh again.

So what, said Eugen.

Naturally, said Gauss, if you didn't think that much, this would seem obvious. As would the fact that young men carry sticks, and old men don't.

Students carry a knobbed stick, said Eugen. It had always been that way and always would be.

Probably, said Gauss, and smiled.

4

They spooned up their soup in silence until the gendarme from the frontier post came in to ask for their passports. Eugen gave him his permit: a certificate from the Court which said that although he was a student he was harmless and was permitted to set foot on Prussian soil if accompanied by his father. The gendarme looked at him suspiciously, inspected the pass, nodded, and turned to Gauss. Gauss had nothing.

No passport, asked the gendarme, astonished, no piece of paper, no official stamp, nothing?

He had never needed such a thing, said Gauss. The last time he crossed the border from Hannover had been twenty years ago. There hadn't been any problems then.

Eugen tried to explain who they were, where they were going, and at whose bidding. The Scientific Congress was taking place under the auspices of the crown. As guest of honor, his father's invitation came, so to speak, directly from the king.

The gendarme wanted a passport.

There was no way he could know, said Eugen, but his father was honored in the most distant countries, he was a member of all Academies, had been known since his first youth as the Prince of Mathematics.

Gauss nodded. People said it was because of him that Napoleon had decided not to bombard Göttingen.

Eugen went white.

Napoleon, repeated the gendarme.

Indeed, said Gauss.

The gendarme demanded his passport again, louder than before.

5

Gauss laid his head down on his arms and didn't move. Eugen nudged him but it did no good. He didn't care, said Gauss, he wanted to go home, he didn't give a hoot.

The gendarme fidgeted uneasily with his cap.

Then the man from the next table joined in. All this would end! Germany would be free, and good citizens would live unmolested and travel sound in mind and body, and would have no further need of bits of paper.

The incredulous gendarme asked for his passport.

That was exactly what he meant, cried the man, and dug around in his pockets. Suddenly, he leapt to his feet, knocking over his chair, and bolted outside. The gendarme gaped at the open door for several seconds before pulling himself together and going in pursuit.

Gauss slowly raised his head. Eugen suggested that they set off again immediately. Gauss nodded and ate the rest of his soup in silence. The little gendarme's hut was empty, both officers having gone after the man with the beard. Eugen and the coachman together pried the barrier up into the air. Then they drove onto Prussian soil.

Gauss was in good order now, almost cheerful, and talking about differential geometry. It was almost impossible to imagine where the investigation into curved space would lead next. Eugen should be glad he was so mediocre, sometimes such questions could be terrifying. Then he talked about how bitter his youth had been. His own father had been hard and dismissive, so Eugen should think himself lucky. He had started to count before he could talk. Once his

6

father had made an error when he was counting out his monthly pay, and this had made Gauss start to cry. As soon as his father caught the mistake, he immediately fell quiet again.

Eugen looked impressed, even though he knew the story wasn't true. His brother Joseph had made it up and spread it around. His father must have heard it recounted so often that he had begun to believe it himself.

Gauss's conversation turned to chance, the enemy of all knowledge, and the thing he had always wished to overcome. Viewed from up close, one could detect the infinite fineness of the web of causality behind every event. Step back and the larger patterns appeared: Freedom and Chance were a question of distance, a point of view. Did he understand?

Sort of, said Eugen wearily, looking at his pocket watch. It didn't keep very good time, but he thought it must be between four-fifty and five in the morning.

But the laws of probability, Gauss went on, pressing both hands against his aching back, weren't conclusive. They were not part of the laws of nature, and there could be exceptions. Take an intellect like his own, for example, or a win at a game of chance, which any simpleton could undeniably pull off at any time. Sometimes he actually theorized that even the laws of physics were merely statistical, hence they allowed for exceptions: ghosts or thought transference.

Eugen asked if this was a joke.

He couldn't answer that himself, said Gauss, closed his eyes, and went into a deep sleep.

They reached Berlin the next day in the late afternoon. Thousands of little houses in a chaotic sprawl, a settlement overflowing its banks in the swampiest spot in Europe. The first splendid buildings were beginning to go up: a cathedral, some palaces, a museum to house the finds from Humboldt's great expedition.

In a few years, said Eugen, this would be a metropolis like Rome, Paris, or St. Petersburg.

Never, said Gauss. Horrible place!

The coach bumped over badly laid cobblestones. Twice the horses shied away from growling dogs, and in the side streets the wheels almost stuck fast in the wet sand. Their host lived in the Packhof at number 4, in the middle of the city, right behind the building site of the new museum. To make sure they didn't miss it, he had drawn a very precise plan with a fine pen. Someone must have seen them from a distance and announced their arrival, for a matter of seconds after they pulled into the courtyard, the main door flew open and four men were running towards them.

Alexander von Humboldt was a little old gentleman with snow-white hair. Behind him came a secretary with an open pad of writing paper, a flunkey in livery, and a young man with whiskers carrying a stand with a wooden box on it. As if rehearsed, they took up their positions. Humboldt stretched out his arms towards the door of the coach.

Nothing happened.

From inside the vehicle came sounds of hectic speech. No, cried someone, no! A dull blow rang out, then a third no! After which there was nothing for a while.

Finally the door swung open and Gauss clambered carefully down into the street. He shrank back as Humboldt seized him by the shoulders and cried what an honor it was, what a great moment for Germany, for science, for him personally.

The secretary was taking notes, and the man behind the wooden box hissed, Now!

Humboldt froze. This was Monsieur Daguerre, he whispered without moving his lips. A protégé of his, who was working on a piece of equipment which would fix the moment on a light-sensitive silver iodide plate and snatch it out of the onrush of time. Please hold absolutely still!

Gauss said he wanted to go home.

Just a moment, whispered Humboldt, a mere fifteen minutes, tremendous progress had been made already. Until recently it had taken much longer, when they tried it first he had thought his back wouldn't hold out under the strain. Gauss wanted to pull himself free, but the little old man held him with surprising strength and murmured, Bring word to the king. The flunkey was off at a run. Then, probably because that was what was going through his mind at that moment: Take a note. Check possibility of breeding seals in Warnemünde, conditions seem propitious, give me proposal tomorrow. The secretary scribbled.

Eugen, who was only just climbing out of the coach with a slight limp, made his apologies for the late hour of their arrival.

There was no late here, and no early, murmured Humboldt. Here there was only work, and the work got done. Luckily it was still light. Not to move.

A policeman entered the courtyard and asked what was going on.

Later, hissed Humboldt, his lips pressed together.

This was an unauthorized gathering, said the policeman. Either everyone went their separate ways or this would become police business.

He was a chamberlain, Humboldt hissed.

Excuse me? The policeman bent forward.

Chamberlain, Humboldt's secretary repeated. Member of the Court.

Daguerre ordered the policeman to get out of the picture.

Frowning, the policeman stepped back. First of all, anyone could claim the same thing, and secondly, the ban on gatherings applied to everyone. And that one there, pointing to Eugen, was clearly a student. Which made it particularly ticklish.

If he didn't immediately make himself scarce, said the secretary, he would find himself in difficulties he couldn't even begin to imagine.

This was no way to address an officer, said the policeman nervously. He would give them five minutes.

Gauss groaned and pulled himself free.

Oh no, cried Humboldt.

Daguerre stamped his foot. Now the moment had been lost forever!

Just like all the others, said Gauss calmly. Like all the others.

10

And indeed, when Humboldt inspected the exposed copper plate with a magnifying glass that same night, while Gauss snored so loudly in the room next door that he was audible throughout the entire apartment, he could recognize absolutely nothing on it. Only after a time did he think he saw a maze of ghostly outlines begin to emerge, the blurred sketch of something like an underwater landscape. In the middle, a hand, three shoes, a shoulder, the cuff of a uniform and the lower portion of an ear. Or then again, not? With a sigh he threw the plate out of the window and heard a dull crash as it landed in the courtyard. Seconds later, like everything else at which he had ever failed, he had forgotten it.

The Sea

Alexander von Humboldt was famous in all of Europe for an expedition to the tropics he had led twenty-five years earlier. He had been in New Spain, New Granada, New Barcelona, New Andalusia, and the United States; he had discovered the natural canal that connects the Orinoco and the Amazon; he had climbed the highest mountain in the known world; he had collected thousands of plants and hundreds of animals, some living, the majority dead; he had talked to parrots, disinterred corpses, measured every river, every mountain, and every lake in his path, had crawled into burrows and had tasted more berries and climbed more trees than anyone could begin to imagine.

He was the younger of two brothers. Their father, a wealthy man of the minor nobility, had died early. When seeking advice on how to educate her sons, his mother had turned to no less a figure than Goethe.

The latter's response was that a pair of brothers in whom the whole panoply of human aspirations so manifested itself, thus promising that the richest possibilities both of action and aesthetic appreciation might become exemplary reality, presented as it were a drama capable of filling the mind with hope and feeding the spirit with much to reflect upon.

Nobody could make head or tail of this sentence. Not their mother, not Kunth the majordomo, a rail of a man with large ears. He took it to mean, he said finally, that it was a kind of experiment. The one should be educated to be a man of culture, and the other a man of science.

And which was which?

Kunth thought. Then he shrugged his shoulders and suggested that they toss a coin.

Fifteen highly paid experts came to lecture them at university level. For the younger brother it was chemistry, physics, and mathematics, for the elder it was languages and literature, and for them both it was Greek, Latin, and philosophy. Twelve hours a day, seven days a week, with no time off and no holidays.

The younger brother, Alexander, was taciturn and frail; he needed encouragement in everything he did and his marks were mediocre. When left to his own devices, he wandered in the woods, collecting beetles and ordering them in categories he made up himself. At the age of nine he followed Benjamin Franklin's design and built a lightning conductor and attached it to the roof of the castle they lived in near the capital. It was only the second anywhere in Germany; the other was in Göttingen, mounted on physics professor Lichtenberg's roof. These were the only two places where one was safe from the heavens.

The elder brother looked like an angel. He could talk like a poet and from the earliest age wrote precocious letters to the most famous men in the country. Everyone who met him was dazzled, almost overcome. By thirteen he had mastered two languages, by fourteen four, by fifteen seven. He had never been punished; nobody could even remember him doing anything wrong. With English envoys he talked about economic policy, with the French the dangers of insurrection. Once he locked his younger brother in a cupboard in a distant room. When a servant found the little boy half-unconscious the next day, he swore he'd locked himself in; he knew nobody would believe the truth. Another time he discovered a white powder in his food. He knew enough about chemistry to identify it as rat poison. With trembling hands he pushed the plate away. From the other side of the table his elder brother watched him knowingly, his pale eyes impenetrable.

Nobody could deny that the castle was haunted. Nothing spectacular, just footsteps in empty corridors, sounds of children crying out of nowhere, and sometimes a shadowy man who asked in a rasping voice to buy shoelaces, little toy magnets, or a glass of lemonade. But the stories about the spirits were even eerier than the spirits themselves. Kunth gave the two boys books to read full of monks and open graves and hands reaching up out of the depths and potions brewed in the underworld and séances where the dead talked to terrified listeners. This kind of thing was just becoming fashionable and was still so novel that there was no familiarity that could inure people to the feelings of horror. And horror was necessary, according to Kunth, encountering the dark side of things was part of growing up; anyone innocent of metaphysical anxiety would never achieve German manhood. Once they stumbled on a story about Aguirre the Mad, who had renounced his king and declared himself emperor. He and his men traveled the length of the Orinoco in a journey that was the stuff of nightmares, past riverbanks so thick with undergrowth that it was impossible to land. Birds screamed in the language of extinct tribes, and when one looked up, the sky reflected cities whose architecture never came from human hands. Hardly any scholars had ever penetrated this region, and there was no reliable map.

But he would, said the younger brother. He would make the journey.

Naturally, the elder brother replied.

He really meant it!

Yes he understood that, said the elder brother and summoned a servant to note down the day and the exact time. The day would come when they would be glad they had fixed this moment.

Their teacher in physics and philosophy was Marcus Herz, Immanuel Kant's favorite pupil and husband of the famed beauty Henriette. He poured two substances into a beaker: the liquid did nothing for a moment, then suddenly changed color. He poured hydrogen out of a little tube, held a flame to its mouth, and there was a joyous explosion of fire. Half a gram, he said, produced a twelve-centimeter flame. Whenever things were frightening, it was a good idea to measure them.

Henriette held a salon every week for intellectual sophisticates who talked of God and their feelings, wept

15

a little, wrote one another letters, and called themselves the Assembled Virtues. No one could remember how this name had come about. Their conversations were kept secret from outsiders, but all impulses of the soul were to be shared completely openly with other Assembled Virtues. If the soul failed to experience impulses, they had to be invented. The two brothers were the youngest. This too was an essential part of their upbringing, said Kunth, and they must never miss a single gathering. It served to educate the emotions. Specifically, he encouraged them to write to Henriette. A neglect of one's sentimental education early in life could bear the most unfortunate fruit. It went without saying that every letter must be shown to him first. As expected, the elder brother's letters were finer.

Henriette's replies were courteous, and written in an unsure child's hand. She herself was barely nineteen. A book that the younger brother had lent to her was returned unread: *Man a Machine* by La Mettrie. A proscribed work, an abominable pamphlet! She could not bring herself to so much as open it.

What a pity, said the younger brother to the elder. It was a notable book. The author was insistent that man was a machine, a highly sophisticated automaton.

And no soul, answered the elder brother. They were walking through a park that surrounded the castle; a thin layer of snow coated the bare trees.

No, the younger boy contradicted him. With a soul. With intimations and a poetic feel for expanse and beauty. Nonetheless this soul itself was no more than a part, even if the most complex one, of the machine.

And he asked himself if this didn't correspond to the truth.

All human beings are machines?

Perhaps not all, said the younger boy thoughtfully. But we are.

The pond was frozen over, and the late afternoon dusk was turning the snow and the icicles to blue. He had something to tell him, said the older boy. People were worried about him. His silences, his reserve. His laborious progress at his lessons. A great experiment would either stand or fall with them. Neither of them had the right to let go of things. He paused for a moment. The ice looks quite solid.

Really?

Yes of course.

The younger boy nodded, took a deep breath, and stepped onto the ice. He wondered if he should recite Klopstock's ode to skating. Arms swinging wide, he glided to the middle and turned in a circle. His brother was standing bent slightly forward on the bank, watching him.

Suddenly everything was silent. He couldn't see anything any more and the cold knocked him almost unconscious. Only now did he realize that he was underwater. He kicked out. His head banged against something hard, the ice. His sheepskin hat came off and floated away, his hair was loose and his feet hit bottom. Now his eyes were accustoming themselves to the darkness. For a moment he saw a frozen landscape: trembling stalks, things growing above them, transparent as a veil, a lone fish, there for a moment then gone, like a hallucination. He made swimming motions, rose in the water, banged into the ice again. He realized he only had a few more seconds to live. He groped, and at the moment when he ran out of air, he saw a dark patch above him, the opening; he dragged himself up, gasped in air, breathed out again and spat, the sharp angles of the ice cut into his hands, he heaved himself out, rolled away, pulling his legs up after him, and lay there, panting and sobbing. Turning onto his stomach, he belly-flopped toward the bank. His brother was still standing there, bent forward the way he had been, hands in his pockets, his cap pulled down over his face. He reached out a hand and helped him to his feet.

That night the fever started. He was aware of voices and didn't know whether they belonged to figures in his dreams or the people who were standing round his bed, and he could still feel the cold of the ice. A man who must be the doctor was pacing up and down the room, and said it's up to you, you'll either make it or you won't, it's your decision, all you have to do is hold on, you know. But when he tried to answer, he could no longer remember what had been said; instead he was looking at the wide expanse of a sea under skies flickering with electricity, and when he opened his eyes again it was noon two days later, the winter sun was hanging all pale in the window and his fever had broken.

From now on his marks improved. He concentrated when he worked and began a habit of balling his fists while thinking, as if there were an enemy to conquer. He had changed, Henriette said in a letter to him, and now he made her a little fearful. He asked permission to spend a night in the empty room which was the most frequent source of nocturnal sounds. In the morning he was white and quiet, and the first vertical line had appeared in his brow.

Kunth decided that the elder brother should study jurisprudence, and the younger, public administration. Of course he traveled with them when they went to university at Frankfurt-on-the-Oder; he accompanied them to lectures and oversaw their progress. It was not a good higher education. If someone incompetent wanted to earn his doctorate, the elder boy wrote to Henriette, he could come here in full confidence. And for some unknown reason there was also a large dog which attended lectures most of the time, scratching incessantly and making noises.

It was the botanist Willdenow who introduced the younger boy to his first dried plants from the tropics. They had protuberances that looked like feelers, buds like eyes, and leaves with upper surfaces that felt like human skin. They seemed familiar to him from his dreams. He dissected them, made careful sketches, tested their reaction to acids and alkalis, and worked them up cleanly into preparations.

He knew now, he said to Kunth, what he wanted to concern himself with: Life.

He couldn't give his approval, said Kunth. One had more tasks on earth than mere existence. Life in and of itself did not supply the content for existence.

19

That wasn't what he'd meant, he replied. He wanted to investigate Life, to understand its strange grip on the world. He wanted to uncover its tricks!

So he was allowed to stay and study with Willdenow. Next semester the elder brother transferred to the University of Göttingen. While he was finding his first friends there, trying his first alcohol, and touching his first woman, the younger boy was writing his first scientific paper.

Good, said Kunth, but not yet good enough to be printed under the name of Humboldt. Publication would have to wait.

During the holidays he visited his elder brother. At a reception given by the French consul, he met Kästner the mathematician, his friend Privy Councilor Zimmerman, and Professor Georg Christoph Lichtenberg, the most important experimental Physicist in Germany. The latter, a hunchback, a clotted mass of flesh and intellect, with a flawlessly beautiful face, pressed his hand softly and stared up at him with a twinkle. Humboldt asked him if it was true he was working on a novel.

Yes and no, said Lichtenberg with a look that suggested he could see something beyond Humboldt's understanding. The work was called *About Gunkel*, had no story, and was making no progress.

Writing a novel, said Humboldt, seemed to him the perfect way to capture the most fleeting essence of the present for the future.

Aha, said Lichtenberg.

Humboldt blushed. It must be a foolish undertaking for an author, as was becoming the fashion these days, to choose some already distant past as his setting.

Lichtenberg observed him with narrowed eyes. No, he said. And yes.

On the way home, the brothers saw a second slice of silver, only slightly larger, alongside the newly risen moon. A hot-air balloon, the elder explained. Pilâtre de Rozier, a collaborator of the Montgolfier brothers, was in nearby Brunswick for the moment. The whole town was talking about it. Soon everyone would be going up in the air.

But they wouldn't want to, said the younger boy. They would be too afraid.

Shortly before leaving, he was introduced to the famous Georg Forster, a thin man with a cough and an unhealthy pallor. He had circumnavigated the globe with Cook and seen more than any German had ever seen; now he was a legend, his book was world-famous, and he worked as the librarian in Mainz. He told tales of dragons and the living dead, of supremely well-mannered cannibals, of days when the sea was so clear that one seemed to be rocking over an abyss, of storms so fierce that one didn't even dare pray. Melancholy enveloped him like a fine mist. He had seen too much, he said. That was the meaning of the simile about Odysseus and the Sirens. It was no good tying oneself to the mast; even when one escaped, one couldn't recover from the brush with the unknown. He could hardly sleep any more, he said, his memories were too strong. Recently he had had the news that his captain, the great saturnine Cook, had been boiled and eaten on Hawaii. He rubbed his forehead and looked at the buckles on his shoes. Boiled and eaten, he said again.

He too wanted to go on voyages, said Humboldt.

Forster nodded. Quite a few had that wish. And everyone of them regretted it later.

Why?

Because one could never come back.

Forster recommended him to the school of mining in Freiberg. It was where Abraham Werner worked. The earth's interior, he taught, was cold and hard. Mountain ranges were created by the chemical precipitations left as the primordial oceans shrank. The fire in volcanoes didn't come from deep in the earth, it was fed by burning coalfields. The core of the earth was solid rock. This theory was called Neptunism and was championed by both churches and Johann Wolfgang von Goethe. In the chapel at Freiberg Werner had masses said for the souls of his opponents who still denied the truth. Once he had broken the nose of a doubting student, and supposedly bitten off the ear of another years before. He was one of the last alchemists: member of secret lodges, expert in the signs that commanded the obedience of demons. He had the power to reassemble what had been destroyed, to re-create what had been burned from its smoke, and to make pulverized objects take shape again; he had also talked to the Devil and made gold. But he didn't give the impression of being an intelligent man. He leaned back, squeezed his eyes shut, and asked Humboldt if he was a Neptunist and believed in a cold earth's core.

Humboldt said yes.

Then he should get married.

Humboldt went red.

Werner puffed out his cheeks, looked conspiratorial, and asked if he had a sweetheart.

That was only an impediment, said Humboldt. One got married when one had nothing essential to do in life.

Werner stared at him.

Or so it was said, added Humboldt hurriedly. Of course that was wrong!

No unmarried man, said Werner, had ever made a good Neptunist.

Humboldt ran through the entire curriculum of the mining school in three months. In the mornings he spent six hours underground, in the afternoons he went to lectures, in the evenings and for half the night he learned what he needed for the next day. He had no friends, and when his brother invited him to his wedding — he had found a woman, he said, who suited him perfectly, there was no one like her in the world — he answered politely that he couldn't come, he had no time. He crawled through the lowest tunnels until he had accustomed himself to his claustrophobia as one would make peace with a relentless pain that slowly became bearable. He measured temperatures: the deeper one went, the warmer it got, which contradicted Abraham Werner's every teaching. He noticed that even in the deepest, darkest caves there was vegetation. Life seemed to have no boundary, some new form of moss or other growth occurred everywhere, or some kind of rudimentary plant. They struck him as sinister, which is why he dissected and examined them, classified them, and wrote an essay on each. Years later, when he saw similar plants in the Cavern of the Dead, he was prepared.

He took the final examinations and was given a uniform. He was supposed to wear it wherever he went. His official title was Assessor in the Department of Mines. He was embarrassed, he wrote to his brother, to be so pleased.

Not many months later he was already the most reliable inspector of mines in Prussia. He went on inspection tours of foundries, peat bogs, and the firing chimneys of the Royal Porcelain Factory; wherever he went, he scared the workers by the speed of his note-taking. He was always on the road, barely ate or slept, and had no idea himself what it was all supposed to be for. There was something in him, he wrote to his brother, that made him afraid he was losing his mind.

By chance he stumbled upon Galvani's book on electrical current and frogs. Galvani had removed the legs from frogs, then attached two different metals to them, and they had twitched as if alive. Was this something inherent in the legs themselves, which retained some life force, or was the movement of external origin, produced by the difference between the metals, and merely made manifest by the frog parts? Humboldt decided to find out.

He took off his shirt, lay down on the bed, and instructed a servant to attach two cupping glasses to his back. The servant obeyed, and Humboldt's skin produced two large blisters. And now please cut the blisters open! The servant hesitated, Humboldt had to raise his voice, the servant took up the scalpel. It was so sharp that the cut caused almost no pain. Blood dripped onto the floor. Humboldt ordered a piece of zinc to be laid on one of the wounds.

The servant asked if he could stop for a moment, he wasn't feeling well.

Humboldt told him not to be so stupid. As a piece of silver touched the second wound, a painful spasm shot through his back muscles and up into his head. With a shaking hand he made a note: *Musculus cucullaris*, ongoing prickling sensation in dorsal vertebrae. No doubt about it, this was electricity! Repeat with the silver! He counted four shocks, regularly spaced, then the objects around him lost their color.

When he regained consciousness, the servant was sitting white-faced on the floor, his hands bloody.

Onward, said Humboldt, and with a strange shiver of apprehension he realized that something in him was finding pleasure in this. Now for the frogs!

Oh no, said the servant.

Humboldt asked if he was intending to look for a new job.

The servant laid four dead, meticulously cleaned frogs on Humboldt's bloodied back. But this was quite enough, he said, after all they were both good Christians.

Humboldt ignored him and ordered silver again. The shocks began immediately. With each one, as he saw in the mirror, the frogs jumped as if alive. He bit down into the pillow, the cloth was wet from his tears. The servant giggled hysterically. Humboldt wanted to make notes, but his hands were too weak. Laboriously he got to his feet. The two wounds were running and the liquid coming out of them was so corrosive it was inflaming his skin. Humboldt tried to capture some of it in a glass tube, but his shoulder was swollen up and he couldn't turn round. He looked at the servant.

The servant shook his head.

Very well, said Humboldt, in that case in God's name would he please get the doctor! He wiped his face and waited until he regained the use of his hands so that he could jot down the essentials. There had been a flow of current, he had felt it, and it hadn't come from his body or the frogs, it had come from the chemical antagonism between the metals.

It wasn't easy to explain to the doctor what had been going on. The servant gave notice the same week, two scars remained, and the treatise on living muscle fiber as a conductor established Humboldt's reputation as a scientist.

He seemed to be showing some evidence of confusion, said his brother in a letter from Jena. He should really bear in mind that one also had moral obligations to one's own body, which wasn't just some random object among many; I'm begging you, do come, Schiller wants to meet you.

You misunderstand me, Humboldt replied, I have established that a human being is prepared to endure insult, but that a great deal of knowledge escapes him because he is afraid of pain. The man who deliberately undergoes pain nonetheless learns things he didn't . . . He laid down his pen, rubbed his shoulder, and crumpled the paper into a ball. Why, I wonder, he began again, does the fact that we are brothers strike me as the real riddle? That the two of us are alone, that we're doubles, that you are what I was never intended to be, and I am what you cannot be, that we must go through existence as a pair, together, whether we want it or not, closer all our lives than either of us will ever be to someone else. And why do I imagine that the greatness we each achieve will have no future, no matter what successes we have, and that it will vanish as if it were nothing until our names, which competed against each other in their fame, melt back into one and fade to a blank? He faltered, then tore the sheet into little pieces.

To examine the plants in the Freiberg mines, he developed the miner's lamp: a flame fed by a gas canister which worked in places even where there was no air. It almost killed him. He climbed down into a chamber in the rock that had never been explored before, set down the lamp, and within a matter of minutes lost consciousness. Dying, he saw tropical creepers which turned to women's bodies as he watched, and came back to his senses with a scream. A Spaniard named Andres del Rio, a former classmate at the Freiberg School of Mines, had found him and got him up to the surface again. Humboldt was almost too ashamed to thank him properly.

It took him a month of hard work to develop a breathing machine: two pipes led from an airbag to a breathing mask. He strapped the apparatus on and went down. Stony-faced he endured the onset of hallucinations. Then first his knees began to buckle and dizziness multiplied the single flame to a blaze; he opened the air valve and watched grimly as the women turned back into plants and the plants into mere nothings. He stayed down in the cool darkness for hours. When he emerged into the daylight, he was met with a letter from Kunth, summoning him to his mother's deathbed.

As was appropriate, he found the fastest horse and rode out. Rain lashed his face, his coat flapped behind him, twice he slipped from the saddle and landed in the dirt. He arrived filthy and unshaven, and because he knew what was correct behavior, he pretended to be out of breath. Kunth nodded his approval; they sat together at her bedside and watched as the pain transformed her face into something unknown. Consumption had burned her up inside, her cheeks had fallen in, her chin was long, and her nose was suddenly hooked; so much blood had been let that she had almost died of it. While Humboldt held her hand, afternoon passed over into evening and a messenger brought a letter from his brother, excusing himself on the grounds of urgent business in Weimar. As night set in, his mother struggled erect in bed and began to emit sharp screams. The sleeping draught was having no effect, even another bleeding brought no relief, and Humboldt could not believe the fact that she was capable of such improper behavior. Around midnight her screams became so unbridled and loud and seemed to be coming from so deep in her body as it arched upward that she seemed to be in ecstasy. He waited with closed eyes. It took two hours for her to fall quiet. At first light, she murmured something incomprehensible; as the sun rose in the morning sky she looked at her son and said he must control himself, that was no way to be lolling about. Then she turned her head away, her eyes seemed to turn to glass, and he was looking at the first corpse he had ever seen in his life.

Kunth put a hand on his shoulder. No one could begin to measure what this family had meant to him.

No, said Humboldt, as if someone were whispering to him, he could measure it and he would never forget.

Kunth was moved, and sighed. Now he knew he would continue to receive his keep.

In the afternoon the servants watched Humboldt walking up and down in front of the castle, over the hills, round the pond, mouth wide open, face turned up to the sky, looking like an idiot. They had never seen him this way. He must surely, they said to one another, be awfully shaken. And he was: he had never been so happy.

A week later he resigned his post. The minister couldn't understand it. Such high office at such a young age, and no limit to how high he might climb! So why?

Because none of it was enough, answered Humboldt. He stood there, a slight figure but ramrod straight, his eyes glistening and his shoulders relaxed, in front of his superior's desk. Because at last he was free to go.

First came Weimar, where his brother introduced him to Wieland, Herder, and Goethe. The latter greeted him as an ally. Any pupil of the great Werner would find a friend in him.

He was going to travel to the New World, said Humboldt. He had never confessed this to anyone before. No one would prevent him, and he didn't expect to come back alive.

Goethe took him aside and led him through a suite of rooms all painted different colors to a high window. A great undertaking, he said. His priority would be to investigate volcanoes, to support the theory of Neptunism. There was no fire under the earth's crust. Nature's heart was not made of boiling lava. Only spoiled minds could seize upon such repellent ideas.

Humboldt promised to take a look at volcanoes.

Goethe crossed his arms behind his back. And he was never to forget where he came from.

Humboldt didn't understand him.

He should think about who had sent him, Goethe gestured toward the brightly colored rooms, the plaster casts of Roman statues, the men who were conversing in lowered voices in the salon. Humboldt's elder brother was discussing the merits of blank verse, Wieland was nodding alertly, Schiller was sitting on the sofa stealing a yawn. You come from us, said Goethe, you come from here. You will still be our ambassador across the seas.

Humboldt journeyed on to Salzburg, where he acquired himself the most expensive arsenal of measuring instruments ever to be possessed by one person. Two barometers for air pressure, a hypsometer to measure the boiling point of water, a theodolite for measuring land, a sextant with an artificial horizon, a foldable pocket sextant, a dipping magnetic needle to establish the force of earth's magnetism, a hydrometer for the relative dampness in the air, a eudiometer for measuring the oxygen levels in the air, a Leyden jar to capture electrical charges, and a cyanometer to measure the blue of the sky. Plus two of these pricelessly costly clocks which recently had started to be produced in Paris. They no longer needed a pendulum, but marked the seconds invisibly with regularly moving springs inside. When handled properly, they kept to Paris time, and if one determined the height of the sun above the horizon and then consulted tables, they made it possible to fix the degree of longitude.

He stayed for a year and practiced. He measured every hill around Salzburg, he took daily measurements of the air pressure, he mapped the magnetic field, he tested the air, the water, the earth, and the color of the sky. He practiced dismantling and reassembling every instrument until he could do it blind, standing on one leg, in rain, or surrounded by a herd of fly-tormented cows. The locals decided he was mad. But that too, he realized, was something he must get used to. Once he tied one arm behind his back for a week, so as to become accustomed to physical insult and pain. Because he was bothered by his uniform, he had another one tailored for him and wore it even to bed. The whole trick was never to let anything get to one, he said to Frau Schobel, his landlady, and asked for another glass of the greenish whey that made him feel sick.

Only after that did he go to Paris, where his brother was now living as a private person, to raise his dazzlingly intelligent children according to a strict system of his own. His sister-in-law couldn't stand him. He spooked her, she said, his constant activity struck her as a form of madness, and most of all, he seemed to her a distorted copy, a caricature even, of her husband.

He couldn't really contradict her, was her husband's reply, and it had never been easy to be so completely responsible for all his brother's follies, or be his brother's keeper.

At the Academy, Humboldt gave lectures on the conductivity of human nerves. He was standing right there in the drizzle on the trampled grass outside the city when the last section of longitude was measured that connected Paris to the Pole. As it was completed, everyone took off their hats and shook hands: one ten-millionth of the distance, captured in metal, would become the unit of all future linear measurements. People wanted to name it "the meter." It always filled Humboldt with exultation when something was measured; this time he was drunk with enthusiasm. The excitement stopped him from sleeping for several nights.

He made enquiries about expeditions. A certain Lord Bristol wanted to go to Egypt, but soon landed in prison as a spy. Humboldt learned that the Directory wanted to send a group of researchers to the South Seas under the command of the great Bougainville, but Bougainville was as old as the hills, stone deaf, sat in a chair of state muttering into thin air and making gestures of command that nobody could make head or tail of. When Humboldt bowed to him, he blessed him with a pontifical hand movement and waved him away. The Directory replaced him with the officer Baudin. This man received Humboldt warmly and promised him everything. Shortly thereafter he disappeared along with all the money the state had given him.

One evening there was a young man sitting on the stairs of the house where Humboldt lived, drinking schnapps out of a silver flask; he cursed violently as Humboldt accidentally trod on his hand. Humboldt apologized and they got to talking. The man's name was Aimé Bonpland, and it turned out he had been hoping to sign on with Baudin. He was twenty-five, tall, a bit ragged, not much scarred by smallpox, and had only one missing tooth, right in front. The two of them looked at each other, and later neither of them would have been able to say whether they had shared an intimation that each was going to be the most important person in the other's life, or whether it just seemed that way in retrospect.

According to Bonpland, he came from La Rochelle and had endured the low skies of the provinces like the roof of a prison. Every day he had wanted to get out, had become a military doctor, but the university wouldn't recognize his title. While he was finishing his final exams, he had studied botany, he loved tropical plants, and now he had no idea what he was going to do. Back to La Rochelle — he'd rather be dead!

Humboldt enquired if he might embrace him.

No, said Bonpland, appalled.

They both had similar things behind them, said Humboldt, and the same ahead of them, and if they got together, who was going to stop them? He put out his hand.

Bonpland didn't understand.

They could go together, Humboldt explained, he needed a traveling companion and he had money.

Bonpland looked at him closely and screwed the lid on the flask.

They were both young, said Humboldt, and they had both made up their minds, and together they would become great. Or didn't Bonpland feel this way?

Bonpland didn't feel this way, but Humboldt's excitement was infectious. For this reason, and also because it was impolite to leave someone standing with outstretched hand, he followed suit, suppressing a yelp of pain: Humboldt's grip was stronger than he would have expected from the little man.

And now what?

Where else, said Humboldt, but Spain of course.

Not much later on, the brothers took leave of each other with the gestures of two monarchs. Humboldt was overcome with embarrassment when strands of his sister-in-law's hair brushed his cheek as they kissed goodbye. He asked if they would see each other again. Of course, said his elder brother. In this world or the next. In the flesh or in the light.

Humboldt and Bonpland mounted their horses and rode away. The amazed Bonpland noticed that his companion was able to refrain from turning round even once until brother and sister-in-law were out of sight.

On the way to Spain, Humboldt measured every single hill. He climbed every mountain. He hammered rock samples off every cliff face. Using his breathing machine he explored every cave back to its farthest chamber. Locals watching him fix the sun through the eyepiece of his sextant decided they were heathen worshippers of the stars and stoned them until they had to leap onto their horses and flee at a gallop — the first couple of times they escaped unscathed, but the third one left Bonpland with a bad if superficial wound.

He began to wonder. Was it really necessary, they were just passing through after all, they were headed for Madrid, and it would be a lot quicker if they made straight there, dammit.

Humboldt thought. No, he said, he was sorry. A hill whose height remained unknown was an insult to the intelligence and made him uneasy. Without continually establishing one's own position, how could one move forward? A riddle, no matter how small, could not be left by the side of the road.

From now on they traveled at night so that he could do his measuring undisturbed. The coordinates on their maps needed to be fixed more precisely than had been done to date. These Spanish maps were inaccurate, Humboldt explained. One wanted to know where exactly one's horse was headed.

But we know that, cried Bonpland. This was the main high road and it went to Madrid. Who needed more than that?

It wasn't a question of the high road, Humboldt replied. It was a question of principle.

As they approached the capital the daylight took on a silvery tint. Soon there were almost no more trees. The middle of Spain was no basin, Humboldt explained. Once again the geographers were wrong. It was much more of a high plateau and had once been an island that towered up out of a prehistoric sea.

Obviously, said Bonpland, taking a pull from his flask. An island.

Madrid was run by the minister Mariano de Urquijo. Everyone knew he was sleeping with the queen. The king was powerless, his children despised him, the country thought him a joke. It couldn't be done without Urquijo, for the colonies were closed to foreigners, and there had never been an exception. Humboldt sought out the Prussian, the Belgian, the Dutch, and the French ambassadors. At night he learned Spanish.

Bonpland asked if he ever slept.

Not if he could help it, replied Humboldt.

After a month, he succeeded in being granted an audience with Urquijo in the Aranjuez palace. The minister was plump, nervous, and full of worries. Because of a misunderstanding, and perhaps also because he had once heard mention of Paracelsus, he thought Humboldt was a German doctor and enquired about an aphrodisiac.

Beg pardon?

The minister led him to a dark corner of the stone hall, laid a hand on his shoulder, and lowered his voice. It wasn't about satisfaction. His power over the land rested on his power over the queen. She was no longer a young woman, nor was he a young man now.

Humboldt blinked and looked out of the window. In the white midday glare the park spread out its unreal symmetry. A jet of water rose sluggishly over a Moorish fountain.

There was still much to do, said Urquijo. The Inquisition was still powerful, there was a long way to go before the abolition of slavery. People were plotting in every corner. He didn't know how long he could hold up. Literally. Was he making himself clear?

Slowly, balling his fists, Humboldt walked over to Urquijo's desk, dipped the quill into the ink, and wrote out a prescription. Cinchona bark from the depths of the Amazon, extract of poppies from central Africa, Siberian moss from the high plains, and a flower that had entered legend from Marco Polo's account of his travels. Make a strong decoction of the above, and draw off the third infusion. Drink slowly, once every two days. It would take years to gather all the ingredients. Hesitantly he handed Urquijo the piece of paper.

Never before had foreigners received such documents. Baron von Humboldt and his assistant were to receive every kind of support. They were to be sheltered, handled well, given access to whatever interested them, and could travel in any ship belonging to the crown.

Now, said Humboldt, they just had to break through the English blockade.

Bonpland asked why the documents talked about an assistant.

No idea, said Humboldt absentmindedly. Some misunderstanding.

Was there time to correct it?

Humboldt said that was a bad idea. Passports like this were a gift from heaven. One didn't question them, one took them and set off.

They took passage on the first frigate that was leaving La Coruña for the tropics. The wind was blowing hard from the west and the seas were heavy. Humboldt sat on deck in a folding chair. He felt freer than he had ever been. Luckily, he wrote in his diary, he was never seasick. Then he had to throw up. But this was a question of will! With utmost concentration, interrupting himself only occasionally to hang over the rail, he wrote three sides on how the departure felt, the night falling over the sea, and the lights of the coast dwindling away in the darkness. He stood beside the captain until daybreak, watching him navigate. Then he fetched his own sextant. Round about noon he began to shake his head. At four in the afternoon he laid his equipment aside and asked the captain why he worked so imprecisely.

He had been doing it for thirty years, said the captain.

With all respect, said Humboldt, that astonished him.

One wasn't doing it for the mathematical exercise, said the captain, one wanted to cross the sea. So one followed the degree of latitude, more or less, and sooner or later, there one was.

But how could one live with it, said Humboldt, grown fractious because of his struggle with seasickness, when accuracy meant nothing?

Easy, said the captain. And besides, this was a free ship. If someone didn't like something, he was welcome to leave.

Shortly before Tenerife, they sighted a sea monster. In the distance, almost transparent against the horizon, the body of a snake rose from the water, coiled itself twice, and stared at them with eyes that showed in the telescope as being made of gemstones. Filaments as thin as beard hair hung down around its jaws. Seconds after it submerged again, everyone thought they must have imagined it. Sea mists, perhaps, said Humboldt, or bad food. He decided not to write anything down.

The ship stayed anchored for two days while they took on fresh supplies. While they were still in harbor, they were surrounded by a group of loose women who reached for them and groped their bodies, laughing. Bonpland wanted to allow himself to be abducted by one of them, but Humboldt called him sharply back to order. One of the women stepped behind him, two naked arms wrapped themselves around his neck, and her hair cascaded over his shoulder. He tried to pull himself loose, but one of her hooped earrings had snagged in one of the clasps of his tailcoat. All the women laughed, and Humboldt didn't know where to put his hands. At last she jumped back, giggling. Bonpland was smiling, too, but when he saw Humboldt's expression, he turned serious again.

There's a volcano over there, said Humboldt, his voice shaking, there's not much time, we can't drag our feet.

They hired two guides and began to climb. Beyond a wood of chestnut trees were ferns, then a sandy plain full of whin and furze. Following Pascal, Humboldt worked out their altitude by measuring the air pressure. They spent the night in a cave that was still filled with snow.

Stiff with cold, they bedded down in the shelter of its entrance. The moon hung small and frozen in the sky, the occasional bat swooped past, and the shadow of the summit was etched on the cloud cover below them.

All of Tenerife, Humboldt explained to their guides, was a single mountain jutting up out of the sea. Didn't this interest them?

Frankly, said one of them, not that much.

Next morning they established that not even the guides knew where they were going. Humboldt asked if they had never even been up here before.

No, said the other guide. Why would they have?

The summit was encircled by a field of scree that made it almost impassable; every time they slipped, stones went rattling down into the valley. One of the guides lost his footing and broke the water bottles. Thirsty, with lacerated hands, they reached the summit. The crater of the volcano had been cold for centuries, its floor covered with petrified lava. The view stretched away to La Palma, Gomera, and the mist-shrouded mountains of Lanzarote. While Humboldt examined the peaks with barometer and sextant, the hostile guides huddled on the ground, and Bonpland, chilled to the bone, stared off into the distance.

In the late afternoon, parched, they reached the gardens of Orotava. Humboldt, stupefied, was face to face with the first plants of the New World. The sight of a hairy spider sunning itself on the trunk of a palm tree filled him with shock and delight. That was when he first noticed the dragon tree.

He turned around, but Bonpland had vanished. The tree was gigantic, and certainly thousands of years old. It had been here before the Spaniards, and before the ancient tribes. It had been here before Christ and Buddha, Plato and Tamburlaine. Humboldt held his watch up to his ear. It carried time within itself as it ticked away, while this tree warded off time: a crag against which its river broke. Humboldt touched the deeply corrugated trunk. High above, the branches opened out, and the twittering of hundreds of birds pierced the air. Tenderly, he stroked the bark. Everything died, every human being, every animal, every moment. Only one thing endured. He laid his cheek against the wood, then drew back and glanced around horrified in case anyone had seen him. He quickly wiped away his tears and went in search of Bonpland.

The Frenchman? An angler down at the harbor pointed toward a wooden hut.

Humboldt opened the door and saw Bonpland's naked back over a naked, brown woman. He slammed the door shut, hurried to the ship, not pausing when he heard Bonpland's running footsteps behind him, nor slowing when Bonpland, his shirt thrown over his shoulder and his trousers over his arm, breathlessly excused himself.

If it ever happened again, said Humboldt, he would consider their collaboration at an end.

Oh come on, Bonpland panted, pulling his shirt on as he ran. Sometimes the feeling just came over a person, was that so hard to understand? Humboldt was a man too.

Humboldt told him to think about his fiancée.

He didn't have a fiancée, said Bonpland, climbing into his trousers. He didn't have anybody!

A man is not a beast, said Humboldt.

Sometimes, said Bonpland.

Humboldt asked if he'd never read Kant.

Frenchmen don't read foreigners.

He didn't want to discuss it, said Humboldt. Any more of it, and they would go their separate ways. Could he accept that?

Good God, said Bonpland.

Could he accept that?

Bonpland murmured something incomprehensible and buttoned his trousers.

Some days later, the ship crossed into the tropics. Humboldt laid aside the fish whose air bladder he had just been dissecting in the dimmed light of an oil lamp, and looked up toward the clearly delineated pinpoints of the Southern Cross. The constellations of the new hemisphere, only partially mapped yet. The other half of earth and sky.

Without warning, they entered a swarm of mollusks. The flow of red jellyfish moving against them was so strong that the ship slowly lost headway. Bonpland fished out two of the creatures. He felt strange, he said. He didn't know why, but something here wasn't right.

Next morning there was an outbreak of fever. It stank abominably belowdecks, the sick moaned at night, and even the open air smelled of vomit. The ship's doctor had brought no cinchona bark: too newfangled, bloodletting was tried and true, and much more effective! A young sailor from Barcelona bled to death after the third round. Another was in such a state of delirium that he tried to fly away, flapping his wings several times before he plunged and would have drowned if they hadn't immediately let down a boat and managed to capture him. While Bonpland lay sick in his hammock, drinking boiling hot rum and incapable of doing any work, Humboldt cut up the two mollusks under the microscope, checked the air pressure, the color of the sky, and the temperature every fifteen minutes, dropped a plumb line every half hour, and entered the results in a thick logbook. This in particular, he explained to Bonpland as the breath rattled in his throat, was no time to give in to weakness. Work helped. Numbers banished disorder, even the disorder of fever.

Bonpland asked him if he himself hadn't felt the tiniest hint of seasickness.

He didn't know. He had decided to ignore it, so he didn't notice. Of course he had to vomit from time to time. But he really didn't pay attention any more.

That evening the next corpse was consigned to the water.

This was making him uneasy, Humboldt told the captain. The expedition couldn't be put at risk by a fever. He had decided not to go with them to Veracruz, but to leave the ship in four days' time.

The captain asked if he was a good swimmer.

Not necessary, said Humboldt, at around 6a.m. in three days they would sight some islands, and a day later they'd reach dry land. He had done the calculations.

The captain asked if there was nothing he could go and carve up.

Wrinkling his brow, Humboldt asked if the captain wanted to make fun of him.

Not at all, but just to remember the gulf between theory and practice. Calculations were splendid in themselves, but this wasn't school exercise, this was the ocean. No one could predict currents and winds. The first sight of land simply didn't lend itself to such precise timing.

In the early morning of the third day, the outlines of a coast began slowly to appear in the mist.

Trinidad, said Humboldt calmly.

Hardly. The captain pointed to his chart.

That wasn't accurate, said Humboldt. The distance between the old and new continents had obviously been calculated erroneously. No one had yet measured the currents with exactitude. If it was acceptable, he would transfer himself to terra firma early tomorrow morning.

They disembarked at the mouth of a large river. Its flow was so powerful that the sea seemed to be made up of foaming freshwater. While three boats transported the cases of their equipment to land, Humboldt, dressed in immaculate Prussian uniform, saluted the captain and took his leave. He was barely in the boat that was carrying them toward the land that swayed sluggishly up ahead before he began to write to his brother to describe the light air, the warm breeze, the coconut trees, and the flamingos. I don't know when this will arrive, but see to it that you get it into the newspaper. The world needs to learn of me. I doubt very much that I am of no interest to it.

The Teacher

If anyone asked the professor about his early memories, he was told that such things didn't exist. Memories, unlike engravings or letters, were undated. One came upon things in one's memory which one sometimes was able, on reflection, to arrange in the right order.

His memory of the afternoon when he had corrected his father as he counted out his pay felt lifeless and secondhand. Maybe he had heard the story too often; it seemed manipulated and unreal. Every other memory had to do with his mother. He fell, she comforted him; he cried, she wiped the tears away; he couldn't sleep, she sang to him; a neighboring boy tried to beat him up, but she saw, ran after him and managed to catch him, trapped him between her knees and hit him in the face until he had to grope his way home, bloodied and deaf. He loved her beyond words. If anything happened to her, he would die. It was no mere figure of speech. He knew he would never survive it. That was how it had been when he was three years old, and thirty years later it was no different.

His father was a gardener, his hands were almost always dirty, he didn't earn much, and when he spoke, it was either to complain or to give orders. A German, he kept saying as he wearily ate his potato soup in the evening, was someone who never lolled. Once Gauss asked, Was that all? Was that all it took to be a German? His father thought it over for so long that it beggared belief. Then he nodded.

His mother was buxom and melancholic, and aside from cooking, washing, dreaming, and weeping, he never saw her do anything. She could neither read nor write. He had become aware quite early on that she was aging. Her skin loosened, her body became shapeless, her eyes steadily lost their sparkle, and every year there were new wrinkles on her face. He knew this happened to everyone, but in her case it was unbearable. She was wasting away before his eyes, and there was nothing he could do.

Most of his later memories were of slowness. For a long time he had believed that people were acting or following some ritual that always obliged them to pause before they spoke or did something. Sometimes he managed to accommodate himself to them, but then it became unendurable again. Only gradually did he come to understand that they needed these pauses. Why did they think so slowly, so laboriously and hard? As if their thoughts were issuing from some machine that had first to be cranked and then put into gear, instead of being living things that moved of their own accord. He noticed that people got angry when he didn't stop himself. He did his best, but often it didn't work.

He was also troubled by the black marks in books which seemed to say something to most grownups, but not to his mother or him. One Sunday afternoon, what are you standing there like that for, boy, he got his father to explain some of it: the thing with the big bar, the thing that stuck out at the bottom, the half circle and the whole circle. Then he stared at the page until the unknown things began to complete themselves of their own accord and suddenly words appeared. He turned the page, this time it went faster, in a few hours he could read and that same evening, the book, which was boring moreover and kept talking about Christ's tears and the repentance of the sinful heart, was finished. He brought it to his mother so that he could explain the marks to her too, but she laughed and shook her head sadly. That was the moment when he grasped that nobody wanted to use their minds. People wanted peace. They wanted to eat and sleep and have other people be nice to them. What they didn't want to do was think.

The teacher in school was called Büttner and liked to beat people. He liked to pretend he was strict and ascetic, and only sometimes did his face betray how much he was enjoying it. His favorite thing was to set them exercises which they had to work at for long periods and still were almost impossible to solve without mistakes, so that at the end there would be an excuse to bring out his stick. It was the poorest area in Brunswick, none of the children here would go on to high school, and no one would ever do anything other than manual labor. He knew that Büttner couldn't stand him. No matter how silent he stayed, and how much he tried to answer slowly like all the others, he could feel Büttner's mistrust, and he knew the teacher was only waiting for a reason to beat him a little harder than the rest.

And then he gave him the reason.

Büttner had told them to add up all the numbers from one to one hundred. It would take hours and was impossible to do, even with the best will in the world, without making a mistake in the addition which would be a cause for punishment. Go, Büttner called, no lolling around, get going, now! Later Gauss would no longer be able to say whether he had been tired that day or simply thoughtless. Whatever the case, he had not been in control of himself and three minutes later was standing with his slate which had one line written on it, in front of the teacher's desk.

So, said Büttner, reaching for his stick. His glance fell on the answer, and his hand froze. He asked what that was supposed to be.

Five thousand and fifty.

What?

Gauss lost his voice, he cleared his throat, and sweated. He only wished he was still in his seat counting like the others who were sitting there with their heads down, pretending not to listen. Adding every number from one to a hundred, that was how you did it. A hundred plus one equals a hundred and one. Ninety-nine plus two equals a hundred and one. Always a hundred and one. Ninety-eight plus three equals a hundred and one. You could do that fifty times. So, fifty times a hundred and one.

Büttner was silent.

Five thousand and fifty, Gauss said again, hoping that for once Büttner would understand. Fifty times a hundred and one equals five thousand and fifty. He rubbed his nose. He was close to tears.

God damn me, said Büttner. Then he said nothing for a long time. The muscles in his face were working; he sucked in his cheeks and stuck out his chin, he rubbed his forehead and tapped his nose. Then he sent Gauss back to his place. He was to sit down, be quiet, and stay behind after school was over.

Gauss drew breath.

One word, said Büttner, and it'll be the stick.

So after the last lesson Gauss appeared in front of the teacher's desk, his head bowed. Büttner demanded his word of honor, swear by the all-seeing God, that he had worked it out by himself. Gauss gave it to him, but when he tried to explain that there was nothing to it, that all you had to do was look at a problem without prejudice or a set way of thinking, and the answer would come of itself, Büttner interrupted him and handed him a thick book. Higher arithmetic: one of his hobby-horses. Gauss was to take it home and go through it. Carefully. One creased page, one stain, one finger mark, and he'd get the stick, so help him God.

Next day he gave the book back.

Büttner asked what that was supposed to mean. Yes it was difficult, but you didn't give up so quickly!

Gauss shook his head and wanted to explain, but couldn't. His nose was running. He had to sniff.

So what was going on?

He'd finished it, he stuttered. It had been interesting, he wanted to say thank you. He stared at Büttner, praying this would be enough.

Nobody was allowed to lie to him, said Büttner. This was the hardest mathematical textbook in German. Nobody could study it in a day, and most particularly not an eight-year-old with a running nose.

Gauss didn't know what he was supposed to say.

Büttner reached uncertainly for the book. He should get ready, because now he was going to ask him questions!

Half an hour later he was staring blank-faced at Gauss. He knew he wasn't a good teacher. He had neither the vocation nor any particular abilities. But this much was clear: if Gauss didn't go on to high school, he, Büttner, would have lived in vain. He looked at him up and down, eyes swimming, then, presumably to control his emotions, grabbed the stick and Gauss received the last beating of his life.

The same afternoon a young man knocked at the door of Gauss's parents' home. He was seventeen, his name was Martin Bartels, he was studying mathematics, and he was working as Büttner's assistant. Might he have a few words with the son of the house?

He only had one son, said Gauss's father, and he was eight years old.

That was the one, said Bartels. Might he have permission to do mathematics with the young gentleman three times a week? He didn't wish to speak of lessons, because the very concept was inappropriate, and here he smiled nervously, when this was an activity from which he might learn more than his pupil.

The father told him to stand up straight. The whole thing was absolute nonsense! He thought for a time. On the other hand, there was really nothing to say against it.

They worked together for a year. At the beginning Gauss enjoyed the afternoons, which broke up the monotony of the weeks, although he didn't have much time for mathematics; what he really would have wanted were Latin lessons. Then things got boring. Granted, Bartels didn't think as laboriously as the others, but he still made Gauss impatient.

Bartels announced that he'd talk to the rector at the high school. If his father would permit, Gauss would be given a free place.

Gauss sighed.

It wasn't right, said Bartels reproachfully, that a child should always be sad!

He thought about this, it was an interesting idea. Why was he sad? Maybe because he could see his mother was dying. Because the world seemed so disappointing as soon as you realized how thinly it was woven, how crudely the illusion was knitted together, how amateurish the stitches were when you turned it over to the back. Because only secrets and forgetfulness could make it bearable. Because without sleep, which snatched you out of reality, it was intolerable. Not being able to look away was sadness. Being awake was sadness. To know, poor Bartels, was to despair. Why, Bartels? Because time was always passing.

Together, Bartels and Büttner persuaded his father that he shouldn't be going to work in the spinning mill, he should be going to high school. The father gave his unwilling consent, along with the advice that he should always stand up straight, no matter what happened. Gauss had already been watching gardeners at work for years, and understood that it wasn't lack of human moral fiber that upset his father, it was the chronic back pain that attended his profession. He got two new shirts and free room and board with the pastor.

High school was a disappointment. There really wasn't much to learn: some Latin, rhetoric, Greek, laughably primitive mathematics, and a little theology. His new classmates were not much smarter than the old ones; the teachers resorted to the stick just as often, but at least they didn't hit as hard. At their first midday meal, the pastor asked him how things were going at school.

Passable, he replied.

The pastor asked him if he found learning hard.

He sniffed and shook his head.

Take care, said the pastor.

Gauss looked up, startled.

The pastor looked at him severely. Pride was a deadly sin!

Gauss nodded.

He should never forget it, said the pastor. Never in his whole life. No matter how clever one was, one must always remain humble.

Why?

The pastor apologized. He must have misunderstood.

Nothing, said Gauss, really — nothing.

On the contrary, said the pastor, he wanted to hear it.

He meant it strictly theologically, said Gauss. God created you the way you were, but then you were supposed to spend your life perpetually apologizing to Him. It wasn't logical.

The pastor theorized that he must be having trouble hearing properly.

Gauss pulled out a very dirty handkerchief and blew his nose. He was sure he must be misunderstanding something, but to him it seemed like a deliberate reversal of cause and effect.

Bartels found a new place for him to board free, with Privy Councilor Zimmerman, a professor at Göttingen University. Zimmerman was a lean, affable man, always looked at him with polite awe, and took him along to an audience with the Duke of Brunswick.

The duke, a friendly gentleman with a twitch in his eyelids, was awaiting them in a room all decorated in gold, with so many candles burning that there were no shadows, only reflections in the mirrored ceiling which created a second room that swayed above their heads, except inside out. Ah, so this was the little genius?

Gauss made a bow, as he had been taught. He knew that there would soon be no more dukes. Then absolute rulers would only exist in books, and the idea that one would stand before such a person, bow, and await his all-powerful word would seem so strange as to be a fairy tale.

Count up something, said the duke.

Gauss coughed, and felt hot and faint. The candles were using up almost all the oxygen. He looked into the flames and suddenly understood that Professor Lichtenberg was wrong, and his phlogiston hypothesis was superfluous. It wasn't some light-producing matter that was burning, it was air itself.

If he might be permitted, said Zimmerman, there was a misapprehension here. The young man was no arithmetical artist. On the contrary, he wasn't even that good at reckoning. But mathematics, as His Highness naturally knew, had nothing to do with the gift of doing addition. Two weeks ago the boy had deduced Bode's law of planetary distances all on his own, followed by the rediscovery of two of Euler's theorems he hadn't met before. He had contributed astonishing things to the setting of the calendar: his formula for working out the correct date for Easter had meantime become standard for the whole of Germany. His achievements in geometry were exceptional. Some of them had already been made public, although naturally under the name of this or that teacher because no one wanted to expose the boy to the corrosive effects of early fame.

He was more interested in things to do with Latin, said Gauss huskily with a frog in his throat. And he knew dozens of ballads by heart.

The duke asked, Did someone just say something?

Zimmerman poked Gauss in the ribs. He begged pardon, the young man's origins were uncouth, his manners left something to be desired. But he would vouch for the fact that a stipendium from the Court was the only thing standing between him and the achievements that would redound to the glory of his country.

So was he saying nobody was going to do any counting right now, asked the duke.

Alas, no, said Zimmerman.

Ah well, said the duke, disappointed. But he should have his stipendium all the same. And come back when he had something to show. He was all for science. His favorite godson, little Alexander, had just left to look for flowers in South America. Maybe what they would be doing here was breeding another fellow just like him! He made a gesture of dismissal, and Gauss and Zimmerman bowed just the way they had practiced as they retreated backwards through the door.

Soon after that, Pilâtre de Rozier came to town. He and the Marquis d'Arlandes had gone up in a basket which the Montgolfiers had attached to a hot-air balloon, and flown five and a half miles over Paris. After they landed, it was said, two men had had to help the marquis walk away, as he was babbling nonsense, insisting that luminous creatures with bosoms and bird's beaks had flown around them. It had taken hours for him to calm down and blame it all on an attack of nerves.

Pilâtre had his own flying machine and two assistants, and was on his way to Stockholm. He had spent the night in one of the cheaper hostelries and was about to set off again when the duke sent word that he would like him to do a demonstration.

Pilâtre said it was a waste of time and inconvenient to boot.

The messenger indicated that the duke was unaccustomed to having his hospitality rejected so vulgarly.

What hospitality, said Pilâtre. He had paid for lodging and just preparing the balloon would cost him two days of travel time.

Perhaps it was possible to talk that way to one's superiors in France, said the messenger, in France anything was possible. But in Brunswick he would do well to reflect before sending him back with any such message.

Pilâtre gave in. He should have known, he said wearily, in Hannover it had been the same and in Bavaria too, for that matter. So in the name of Christ he would go up in his balloon tomorrow afternoon in front of the gates of this filthy town.

Next morning there was a knock at his door. A boy was standing outside, looking up at him intently, and asked if he could fly with him.

Travel with him, said Pilâtre. In a balloon, it's travel. You don't say fly, you say travel. That was what balloonists said.

What balloonists?

He was the first, said Pilâtre, so it was his to decree. But no, of course nobody could travel with him. He tickled the boy's cheeks and tried to close the door.

This wasn't the way he usually behaved, said the boy, wiping his nose on the back of his hand. But his name was Gauss, he wasn't some nobody, and before long he would be making discoveries that would equal Isaac Newton's. He wasn't saying this out of vanity, but because time was getting short and he had to be part of the flight. You could see the stars much better up there, couldn't you? Clearer, and not obscured by the haze?

He could bet on it, said Pilâtre.

That's why he had to go too. He knew a lot about stars. You could test him on it as much as you wanted.

Pilâtre laughed and asked who had taught this little man to talk so well. He thought for a while. All right, he said finally, since it was about the stars . . .

That afternoon, before a throng of people, the duke, and a saluting battalion of guests, a fire gradually filled the parchment sac with heat through two tubes. No one had expected it to take so long. Half the spectators had already left when the balloon filled out, and barely a quarter were still there when it started to move upright and jerkily began to lift off the ground. The ropes went taut, Pilâtre's assistants loosened the knots, the little basket moved, and Gauss, huddling on the woven bottom of the basket and whispering to himself, would have leapt to his feet if Pilâtre hadn't pushed him down again.

Not yet, he panted. Are you praying?

No, Gauss whispered, he was counting prime numbers. That's what he always did when he was nervous.

Pilâtre stuck up a thumb to check the direction of the wind. The balloon would rise, then head wherever the wind took it, before sinking again when the air inside it cooled. A seagull shrieked somewhere close to the basket. Not yet, yelled Pilâtre, not yet. Not yet. Now! And seizing him partly by his collar, partly by his hair, he hauled Gauss up.

The curve of the earth in the distance. The deep horizon, the hilltops half-hidden in mist. The people staring upward, tiny faces in a ring around the still-burning fire, and next to them the roofs of the town. Little clouds of smoke, tethered to chimneys. A path snaked through the green, and on it a donkey the size of an insect. Gauss clung on to the rim of the basket and it was when he closed his mouth that he realized he had been screaming.

This is how God sees the world, said Pilâtre.

He wanted to say something back, but he'd lost his voice. How fiercely the air was shaking them! And the sun — why was it so much brighter up here? His eyes hurt, but he couldn't close them. And space itself: a straight line from every point to every other point, from this roof to this cloud, to the sun, and back to the roof. Points making lines, lines making planes, planes making bodies, and that wasn't all. The fine curve of space was almost visible from here. He felt Pilâtre's hand on his shoulder. Never go down again. Up and then up further, until there would be no earth beneath them any more. One day this is what people would experience. Everyone would fly then, as if it were quite normal, but by then he would be dead. He peered excitedly into the sun, the light was changing. Dusk seemed to be rising in the still-bright sky like fog. A last flame or two, red on the horizon, then no more sun, then stars. Things never happened this fast down there.

We've started to drop, said Pilâtre.

No, he begged, not yet! There were so many of them, more every moment. Each one a dying sun. Every one of them was decaying, and they were all following their own trajectories, and just as there were formulae for every planet that circled its own sun and every moon that circled its own planet, there was a formula, certainly infinitely complicated, but then again maybe not, perhaps hiding behind its own simplicity, that described all these movements, every revolution of every individual body around every other; maybe all you had to do was keep looking. His eyes smarted. It felt as if he hadn't blinked for a long time.

We're about to land, said Pilâtre.

No, not yet! He rose on tiptoes, as if that could help, stared upward, and understood for the first time what movement was, what a body was; most of all, what space was, the space that they stretched between them, and that held them all, even him, even Pilâtre and this basket, in its embrace. Space, that . . .

They crashed into the wooden frame of a haystack, a rope tore, the basket tipped over. Gauss rolled into a mud puddle, Pilâtre fell so awkwardly that he sprained his arm, and when he saw the tear in the parchment skin, he began to curse so dreadfully that the farmer who had come running out of his house stopped dead and raised his spade threateningly. The assistants

60

arrived breathless to fold the crumpled balloon together. Pilâtre nursed his arm and gave Gauss a slap that was hard enough to hurt.

Now he knew, said Gauss.

What?

That all parallel lines meet.

Fine, said Pilâtre.

His heart was racing. He wondered if he should explain to the man that all he would need was to add a hanging rudder to the basket, and he could turn the air current to make the balloon move in any specific direction. But he kept quiet. Nobody had asked him, and it wouldn't be polite to force his ideas on these people. It took no stretch of the imagination, and one of them would think of it soon.

But now what this man wanted to see was a grateful child. With an effort, Gauss put a smile on his face, stretched his arms wide, and bowed like a marionette. Pilâtre was happy, laughed, and stroked his head.

The Cavern

After six months in New Amsterdam, Trinidad, Humboldt had examined everything that lacked the feet and the fear to run away from him. He had measured the color of the sky, the temperature of lightning flashes, and the weight of the hoar-frost at night, he had tasted bird droppings, investigated earth tremors, and had climbed down into the Cavern of the Dead.

He lived with Bonpland in a white wooden house on the edge of the town, which had recently suffered earthquake damage. Aftershocks still jolted people awake at night, and when they went to bed and held their breath, they could still hear movement deep down beneath them. Humboldt dug holes, dropped thermometers on long threads down wells, and put peas on drumheads. The quake would certainly begin again, he said cheerfully. Soon the whole town would be in ruins.

In the evenings they ate at the governor's mansion and afterwards there was bathing. Chairs were set down in the river, they put on light clothes and sat in the current. Now and then small crocodiles swam by. Once a fish bit off three toes of the viceroy's nephew. The man, his name was Don Oriendo Casaules and he had a huge mustache, twitched and stared blankly in front of him for a few moments before pulling his now-less-than-whole foot disbelievingly out of the red water. He glanced around as if searching for something, then fell sideways and was caught by Humboldt. The next ship took him back to Spain.

Women were frequent visitors: Humboldt counted the lice in their plaited hair. They came in groups, whispered to one another, and giggled at the little man in his uniform with the magnifying glass firmly clamped in his left eye. Bonpland was made miserable by their beauty. He wanted to know what statistics about lice were good for.

One wanted to know, said Humboldt, because one wanted to know. Nobody had yet investigated the presence of these remarkably resistant creatures on the heads of inhabitants of equatorial regions.

Not far from their house, people were auctioned off. Muscular men and women with chained ankles stared empty-eyed at local landowners as they probed inside their mouths, peered into their ears, and went down on their knees to touch their anuses. They felt the soles of their feet, pulled their noses, checked their hair, and fingered their genitalia. Most of them left afterwards, without buying; it was a shrinking branch of the economy. Humboldt bought three men and had their chains removed. They didn't understand. They were now free, Humboldt said through an interpreter, they could go. They stared at him. Free? One of them asked where they were supposed to go. Wherever you wish, said Humboldt. He gave them money. Cautiously they tested the coins with their teeth. One of them sat down on the ground, closed his eyes, and didn't stir, as if there were absolutely nothing in the world to interest him. Humboldt and Bonpland moved away under the mocking eyes of the bystanders. A couple of times they turned around, but none of the freed men was looking after them. In the evening it began to rain, and that night the town was shaken by a fresh earthquake. Next morning the three men had disappeared. No one knew where, and they never turned up again. When the next auction took place, Humboldt and Bonpland stayed at home, working behind closed shutters, and only went outside after it was over.

The journey to the Chaymas mission led through thick forests. At every stop they saw plants they'd never seen before. The ground seemed not to have enough room for so much growth: tree trunks squeezed against one another, plants clambered over other plants, lianas swept over their heads and shoulders. The monks of the mission greeted them warmly, although they didn't understand what the two men wanted of them. The abbot shook his head. There must be something else behind it! Nobody traveled halfway round the world to measure land that didn't even belong to him.

The mission was home to baptized Indians, who lived under their own self-government. There was an Indian commandant, a chief of police, and even a militia, and provided they obeyed all the rules, they were allowed to live as if they were free. They were naked, wearing only individual items of clothing they had picked up here or there: a hat, a stocking, a belt, an epaulette tied securely to a shoulder. It took Humboldt some while to behave as if he were accustomed to this. It offended him to see that women had hair in so many places; it struck him as incompatible with natural dignity. But when he said as much to Bonpland, the latter looked at him with such amusement that he turned red and began to stutter.

Not far from the mission was the cavern of the night birds, where the dead lived. Because of the old legends, the natives refused to go with them. It took a lot of persuasion before two monks and an Indian would come along. It was one of the longest caverns on the continent, a hole sixty feet by ninety which let in so much light that for the first hundred and fifty feet inside the rock, there was grass underfoot and treetops overhead. Only after that did they need to light torches. This was also where the screaming began.

The darkness was home to birds. Thousands of nests hung from the roof like pouches, and the noise was deafening. How they navigated was a mystery. Bonpland fired three shots which were drowned out by the screeching, and immediately picked up two bodies, still twitching. Humboldt hammered samples of stone out of the rock, measured temperature, air pressure, and relative dampness, and scratched moss off the wall. A monk cried out as his sandal squashed a huge unprotected snail. They had to wade through a stream as the birds fluttered around their heads, and

Humboldt pressed his hands over his ears while the monks made the sign of the cross.

Here, said the guide, was where the kingdom of the dead began. This was as far as he would go.

Humboldt offered to double his pay.

The guide declined. This place was no good! And besides, what were they looking for here; men belonged in the light.

Well said, roared Bonpland.

Light, yelled Humboldt, light wasn't brightness, light was knowledge!

He went on, and Bonpland and the monks followed. The passage divided, and without a guide they didn't know which way to go. Humboldt suggested they split up. Bonpland and the monks shook their heads.

Then left, said Humboldt.

Why left, said Bonpland.

Well then, right, said Humboldt.

But why right?

Dammit, yelled Humboldt, this was becoming really stupid. And he went left, ahead of the others. The screaming of the birds echoed even louder down here. After a time it was possible to make out high-pitched clicking sounds, produced one after the other at great speed. Humboldt knelt down to inspect the misshapen plants on the cave floor. Bloated, colorless growths, almost formless. Interesting, he shouted in Bonpland's ear, he had written a paper in Freiberg about exactly this!

When the two of them looked up, they noticed that the monks were no longer there.

Superstitious blockheads, cried Humboldt. Onward!

The ground sloped sharply downhill. They were surrounded by the clattering of wings, yet no creature ever brushed against them. They groped their way along a wall to a rock cathedral. The torches, too feeble to illuminate the vault, threw exaggerated shadows onto the walls. Humboldt looked at the thermometer: it was getting steadily warmer, he doubted Professor Werner would be pleased! The next thing he saw was the figure of his mother, standing next to him. He blinked, but she remained visible for longer than was appropriate for an illusion. Her shawl tied tight against her throat, head to one side, smiling absentmindedly, chin and nose as thin as they had been on the last day of her life, a bent umbrella in her hands. He closed his eyes and counted slowly to ten.

What did you say, asked Bonpland.

Nothing, said Humboldt, and concentrated on hammering a splinter out of the stone.

Further back there, the passage continued, said Bonpland.

They'd done enough, said Humboldt.

Bonpland offered up that there must surely be more unknown plants deeper inside the mountain.

Better to turn back, said Humboldt. Enough was enough.

They followed a stream in the direction of the sunlight. Gradually the number of birds diminished, their screaming quieted, and soon they could extinguish the torches.

In front of the cave mouth the Indian guide was turning their two birds over a fire to render the fat. The feathers, beaks, and necks were already scorched, blood was dripping into the flames, the fatty tissue was hissing, and a bigger smoke hung over the clearing. The best fat, he explained. Odorless, and it would stay fresh for more than a year.

Now they would need two more, said Bonpland, furious.

Humboldt asked Bonpland for his brandy flask, took a big swallow, and set off on the path back to the mission with one of the monks, while Bonpland returned the other way to shoot two more birds. After several hundred yards, Humboldt stopped still, tilted his head back, and looked up into the treetops which were holding up the sky high above his head.

Reverberation!

Reverberation, repeated the monk.

If it wasn't a sense of smell, said Humboldt, it must be the resonance. That clicking, echoing back off the walls. That must be how the creatures worked out their direction.

As he went on, he made notes. A system that people could utilize on moonless nights or underwater. And the fat: its odorlessness would make it ideal for manufacturing candles. He threw open the door to his monastery cell, and a naked woman was there waiting for him. At first he thought either she was there because of the lice, or she'd brought a message. Then he understood that this time it wasn't the case, and she wanted exactly what he thought she wanted, and that there was no way out.

Obviously the governor had sent her, it fit with his idea of a rough joke between men. She had been waiting alone in the room for a night and a day, out of sheer boredom she'd taken the sextant to pieces and muddled up all the collected plants, drunk the spirits intended for the preparation of specimens, and then slept off her drunkenness. After waking up she'd found a funny portrait of a dwarf with pursed lips, which she naturally failed to recognize as Frederick the Great, and colored it in quite well. Now that Humboldt was finally here, she wanted to get it over with.

While he was still asking where she'd come from, what she wanted, and if there was anything he could do for her, she was already undoing his trousers with a practiced hand. She was small and plump and couldn't be much older than fifteen. He moved backwards, she followed him, he bumped against the wall and as he tried sharply to set her straight, he found he'd forgotten his Spanish.

Her name was Ines, she said, and he could trust her.

As she pulled up his shirt, a button tore off and rolled across the floor. Humboldt followed it with his eyes until it hit the wall and fell over. She put her arms round his neck and pulled him, while he murmured that she was to let go, he was an official of the Prussian Crown, into the middle of the room.

Oh God, she said, listen to your heart pound.

She dragged him down with her onto the carpet, and for some reason he allowed her to roll him onto his back while her hands wandered down over him until she stopped, laughed, and said there wasn't much going on. He looked at her bent back, the ceiling, and the palm leaves shivering in the wind outside the window.

Now, she said. He was to trust her!

The leaves were short and pointed, it was a tree he had never inspected until now. He wanted to sit up, but she laid her hand on his face and pushed him down, and he asked himself how she could fail to understand that he was in hell. Later on he couldn't have said how long it lasted before she gave up, pushed back her hair, and looked at him sadly. He closed his eyes. She stood up.

It didn't matter, she said quietly, it was her fault.

His head hurt, and he had a raging thirst. Only when he heard the door shut behind her did he open his eyes.

Bonpland found him at his desk, surrounded by the chronometers, the hygrometer, the thermometer, and the reassembled sextant. Magnifying glass clenched in his eye, he was looking at palm leaves. Interesting structure, remarkable! It was getting to be time they moved on.

So suddenly?

According to old reports, there was a natural channel between the great rivers of the Orinoco and the Amazon. European geographers took that to be mere legend. The dominant school of theory held that only mountain ranges could act as watersheds, and there was no possible linkage between inland river systems.

Oddly enough, he had never thought about it, said Bonpland.

The theory was wrong, said Humboldt. He was going to find the channel and solve the riddle.

Aha, said Bonpland. A channel.

He didn't like his attitude, said Humboldt. Always complaining, always objecting. Would it be too much to ask for a little enthusiasm?

Bonpland asked if something had happened.

There was about to be an eclipse of the sun! This would enable him to establish the exact coordinates of their coastal town. Then it would be possible to construct a net of measuring points all the way to the end of the channel.

But that would be way deep in primeval forest!

Primeval was a big word, said Humboldt. It shouldn't be allowed to frighten him. Primeval forest was still just forest. Nature spoke the same language everywhere.

He wrote to his brother. The journey was magnificent, with a plethora of discoveries. New plants cropped up every day, more than one could count, and his observations of tremors were suggesting a new theory of the earth's crust. His knowledge of the nature of head lice was also becoming unusually advanced. Yours as always, please put this in the newspaper!

He checked to see if his hand was still trembling. Then he wrote to Immanuel Kant. A new concept of the science of physical geography was forcing its way into his mind. At different altitudes, although at similar temperatures, similar plants grew all over the planet, so climate zones stretched not just laterally but also vertically: at some given spot the earth's surface could thus run the gamut from tropical to arctic. If one connected these zones into lines, one would get a map of the major climate currents. Thanking him for any comments, and in warmest hopes that the professor was in good health, he remained his humble . . . He closed his eyes, inhaled deeply, and signed with the boldest signature he could muster.

The day before the eclipse something unpleasant occurred. As they were taking air pressure measurements down on the beach, a Zambo, part black, part Indian, leapt out of the bushes clutching a wooden club. He growled, hunched his body, stared, and then attacked. An unhappy accident, Humboldt called it, as he wrote his account by flickering candlelight at around 3a.m. some days later on board ship to Caracas in a wild sea. He had ducked left away from the blow, but Bonpland on his right had not been so lucky. But as Bonpland remained lying motionless on the ground, the Zambo missed his opportunity; instead of going for Bonpland again, he had chased after Bonpland's hat as it flew off, and strode away while putting it on his head.

At least no damage to the instruments was incurred and even Bonpland came to after twenty hours: face swollen, one lost tooth, the shape of his nose somewhat altered, and dried blood around mouth and chin. Humboldt, who had been sitting by his bed through the evening, night, and long hours of the morning, handed him some water. Bonpland washed himself, spat, and looked mistrustfully into the mirror.

The eclipse of the sun, said Humboldt. Would he manage?

Bonpland nodded.

Was he sure?

Bonpland spat and said thickly that he was sure.

Great days were coming, said Humboldt. From the Orinoco to the Amazon. Into the heart of the interior. Bonpland must give him his hand!

With great effort, as if pushing against some force of resistance, Bonpland raised his arm.

At the predicted time in the afternoon, the sun was extinguished. The light faded, a swarm of birds flew up into the air, screeching, and swooped away, objects seemed to absorb the brightness, a shadow fell across them, and the ball of the sun became a dark curve. Bonpland, head bandaged, held the screen of the artificial horizon. Humboldt set up the sextant on it, and used the other eye to squint at the chronometer. Time stood still.

And started to move again. The light returned. The ball of the sun emitted rays again, the shadow detached itself from the hills, the earth, then the horizon. Birds called, someone somewhere fired a shot. Bonpland let down the screen.

Humboldt asked what it had been like.

Bonpland stared at him in disbelief.

He hadn't seen any of it, said Humboldt. Only the projection. He had had to fix the constellations in the sextant and also track the exact time. There had been no time to look up.

There wouldn't be a second chance, said Bonpland hoarsely. Had he really not looked up?

This place was now fixed forever in the maps of the world. There were only ever a few moments in which one could use the sky to correct clock time. Some people took their work more seriously than others!

That could well be, but . . . Bonpland sighed.

Yes? Humboldt leafed in the astronomical almanac, took up his pencil, and began to calculate. So what was it now?

Did one always have to be so German?

Numbers

On the day everything changed, one of his molars was hurting so much he thought he'd go insane. In the night he had lain on his back, listening to the landlady snoring next door. At about six thirty in the morning, as he blinked wearily into the dawn light, he discovered the solution to one of the oldest problems in the world.

He went staggering through the room like a drunk. He must write it down immediately, he must not forget it. The drawer didn't want to open, suddenly the paper had hidden itself from him, his quill broke off and made blotches, and then the next thing to trip him up was the chamber pot. But after half an hour of scribbling there it all was on some crumpled piece of paper, the margins of a Greek textbook, and the tabletop. He laid his pen aside. He was breathing heavily. He realized that he was naked, and registered the dirt on the floor and the stink with surprise. He was freezing. His toothache was almost unbearable.

He read. Worked his way through it, followed the proof line by line, looked for errors, and didn't find any. He roamed over the last page and looked at his distorted, smeared, seventeen-sided figure. For more than two thousand years, people had been constructing regular triangles and pentangles with ruler and compasses. To construct a square or to double the angles of a polygon was child's play. And if one combined a triangle and a pentangle, what one got was a fifteen-sided figure. More was impossible.

And now: seventeen. And he had a hunch there was a method that would allow him to go further. But he would have to find it.

He went to the barber, who tied his hands tight, promised it really wouldn't be bad, and with one quick movement pushed his pincers into his mouth. The very touch of them, a blinding flash of pain, almost made him faint. He tried to gather his thoughts, but then the pincers took hold, something went *click* in his head, and it was the taste of blood and the pounding in his ears that brought him back to the room and the man with the apron, who was saying it hadn't been so bad, had it?

On his way home he had to lean against walls, his knees were weak, his feet weren't under control, and he felt dizzy. In another few years there would be doctors for teeth, then it would be possible to cure this kind of pain and you wouldn't have to have every inflamed tooth pulled. Soon the world would no longer be full of the toothless. And everybody wouldn't have pockmarks, and nobody would lose their hair. He was amazed that nobody else ever thought about these things. People thought everything was naturally the way it was. Eyes glazed, he made his way to Zimmerman's rooms.

Entering without knocking, he laid the pieces of paper out in front of him on the dining table.

Oh, said the professor sympathetically, teeth, bad? He himself had been lucky, he'd only lost five, Professor Lichtenberg was left with a mere two, and Kästner had been toothless for years. With the tips of his fingers, because of a bloodstain, he picked up the first sheet. His brow furrowed. His lips moved. It went on so long that Gauss could hardly believe it any more. Nobody could take that long to think!

This is a great moment, said Zimmerman finally.

Gauss asked for a glass of water.

He felt like praying. This must be printed, and it would be best if it appeared under the name of a professor. It wasn't the done thing for students to be publishing on their own.

Gauss tried to reply, but when Zimmerman brought him the glass of water, he could neither speak nor drink. He made a gesture of apology, wobbled home, lay down in bed, and thought about his mother up there in Brunswick. It had been a mistake to come to Göttingen. The university here was better, but he missed his mother, and even more so when he was ill. At about midnight, when his cheek had swollen still further and every movement in every part of his body hurt, he realized the barber had pulled the wrong tooth.

Luckily the streets were still empty in the early morning so nobody saw him stopping continually to lean his head against the house walls and sob. He would have given his soul to live a hundred years later when there would be medications for pain and doctors who deserved the name. Nor was it that hard. All that was necessary was to numb the nerves in the right spot, the best thing would be little doses of poison. Curare needed to be researched better! There was a flask of it in the Institute of Chemistry, he would go and have a look. But his thoughts slid away from him and he was only more aware of his own groaning.

It happens, said the barber cheerfully. Pain spread itself wide, but Nature was intelligent and man came with plenty of teeth. At the moment when he pulled the tooth, everything around Gauss went black.

As if the pain had wiped the event from his memory or from time itself, he found himself hours or days later — how could he tell — back in the chaos of his bed, with a half-empty bottle of schnapps on the night table and at his feet the *Universal Advertiser* and *Literary Supplement*, in which Privy Councilor Zimmerman laid out the latest method for constructing a regular seventeen-sided figure. And sitting beside the bed was Bartels, who had come to congratulate him.

Gauss fingered his cheek. Oh, Bartels. He knew all about it. He himself came out of poverty, had been considered a wunderkind, and believed himself chosen for great things. Then he had met him, Gauss. And he knew, meanwhile, that for the next two nights after they met, Bartels had lain awake and thought about whether he should go back to the village, milk cows, and muck out stalls. Sometime during the third night, he had realized that there was only one way to save himself: he would have to like Gauss. He would have to help him, no matter where it led. From that moment on, he had thrown all his strength into working with Gauss, he had talked to Zimmerman, written letters to the duke, and one difficult evening, by means of threats none of them wanted to remember, he had got Gauss's father to agree to let his son go to high school. And the next summer he had gone with Gauss to visit his parents in Brunswick. Suddenly the mother had taken him aside, her face small with worry and shyness, to ask if there was any future for her son at the university with all the educated people. Bartels hadn't understood. What she meant was, did Carl have any future researching things? She was asking in confidence, and promised not to repeat anything. As a mother, one always had worries. Bartels had remained silent for a while, before asking with a contempt which shamed him later if she didn't know that her son was the greatest scientist in the world. She had wept and wept, and it had been extremely embarrassing. Gauss had never succeeded in forgiving Bartels.

He had come to a decision, said Gauss.

For what? Bartels looked up distractedly.

Gauss gave an impatient sigh. For mathematics. Until now he had wanted to concentrate on classical philology, and he still liked the idea of writing a commentary on Virgil, in particular Aeneas' descent to the underworld. He felt that nobody yet had correctly understood this chapter. But there would still be time for that, after all he had only just turned nineteen. But above all he had realized that he could achieve more in mathematics. If one had to be born, even if nobody had bothered to ask, then one could at least try to accomplish something. For example, solving the question of what a number is. The foundation of arithmetic.

A life's work, said Bartels.

Gauss nodded. With a little luck he'd be finished in five years.

But soon he realized it would go faster than that. Once he had begun, ideas came crowding in with a force he hadn't experienced before. He barely slept, he stopped going to the university, ate the bare minimum, and rarely went to visit his mother. When he wandered through the streets murmuring to himself, he felt he had never been so awake. Without looking where he was going, he avoided bumping into people, he never stumbled, once he leapt to one side for no reason at all and wasn't even surprised when a roof tile landed in the same second at his feet and shattered. Numbers didn't seduce one away from reality, they brought reality closer, made it clearer and more meaningful in a way it had never been before.

Numbers were his constant companions now. He thought of them even when he was visiting whores. There weren't that many in Göttingen, they all knew him, greeted him by name, and sometimes gave him a discount because he was young, good-looking, and well-mannered. The one he liked best was called Nina and came from a distant town in Siberia. She lived in the old lying-in house, was dark-haired, with big dimples in her cheeks and broad shoulders that smelled of the earth; when he was holding her tight, looking up at the ceiling as he felt her rocking on him, he promised he would marry her and learn her language. She laughed at him, and when he swore that he meant it, she answered that he was still very young.

The examination for his doctorate was supervised by Professor Pfaff. In response to his scribbled request, he was exempted from the oral exam, as it would have been quite risible. When he went to collect the document itself, he had to wait in the corridor. He ate a piece of dry cake and read the *Göttingen Scholars' Bulletin*, which contained a report by a German diplomat about his brother's visit to New Andalusia. A white house on the edge of town, evenings cooling off in the river, women who came frequently to visit to have their lice counted. He turned the pages with a vague excitement. Naked Indians in the Chaymas mission, birds that lived in caves and used their voices to see, the way other creatures use eyesight. The great eclipse of the sun, then the departure for the Orinoco. The man's letter had taken eighteen months to arrive, and only God knows whether he was still alive. Gauss lowered the newspaper, Zimmerman and Pfaff were standing in front of him. They hadn't dared to disturb him.

That man, he said, impressive! But crazy too, as if truth was something you found out there and not here. Or as if you could run away from yourself.

Pfaff hesitantly handed him the document: passed, *summa cum laude*. Of course. People were saying, said Zimmerman, that some great work was in progress. He was delighted that Gauss had found something that could occupy his interest and dispel his melancholy.

Yes, he was working on something of the kind, said Gauss, and when it was done, he would be going.

The two professors exchanged glances. Leaving the Electorate of Hannover? They did hope not.

No, said Gauss, please not to worry. He would be going far, but not out of the Electorate of Hannover.

The work advanced quickly. The law of quadratic reciprocity was worked out, and the riddle of the frequency of prime numbers came closer to a solution. He had completed the first three sections and was already into the main part. But again and again he laid his quill aside, propped his head in his hands, and wondered whether there was a proscription against what he was doing. Was he digging too deep? At the base of physics were rules, at the base of rules there were laws, at the base of laws there were numbers; if one looked at them intently, one could recognize relationships between them, repulsions or attractions. Some aspects of their construction seemed incomplete, occasionally hastily thought out, and more than once he thought he recognized roughly concealed mistakes — as if God had permitted Himself to be negligent and hoped nobody would notice.

Then the day came when he had no more money. As he was no longer a student, his stipendium had run out. The duke had never been pleased that he had gone to Göttingen, so there was no question of an extension.

He could get relief, said Zimmerman. By chance there was a job, a temporary one; they needed an industrious young man to help with land surveying.

Gauss shook his head.

It wouldn't last long, said Zimmerman. And fresh air never hurt anybody.

Which was how he found himself unexpectedly stumbling through the countryside in the rain. The sky was low and dark, the earth was muddy. He climbed over a hedge and landed panting, sweating, and strewn with pine needles in front of two girls. Asked what he was doing here, he nervously expounded the technique of triangulation: if you knew one side and two angles of a triangle, you could work out the other sides and the unknown angle. So you picked a triangle somewhere out here on God's good earth, measured the side that was most easily accessible, and then used this gadget to establish the angle of the third corner. He lifted the theodolite and turned it this way, and then this way, and do you see, like this, with awkward fingers, as if doing it for the first time. Then you fit together a whole series of these triangles. A Prussian scientist was in the process of doing exactly this among all the fabulous creatures in the New World.

But a landscape isn't a flat surface, retorted the bigger of the two.

He stared at her. There had been no pause. As if she had needed no time to think it over. Certainly not, he said, smiling.

A triangle, she said, had one hundred and eighty degrees as the sum of its angles on a flat surface; but it was on a sphere, so this was no longer true. Everything would stand or fall based on that.

He looked her up and down as if seeing her for the first time. She returned his look with raised eyebrows.

Yes, he said. So. In order to even things out, you had to scrunch the triangles, so to speak, after measuring them until they were infinitely small. In and of itself, a simple exercise in differentials. Although in this form . . . He sat down on the ground and took out his pad. In this form, he murmured, as he began making notes, it's never been worked out in this form yet. When he looked up, he was alone.

For several weeks he went on crisscrossing the region with the geodetic implements, ramming stakes into the ground and measuring their relative distances. Once he rolled down a slope and dislocated his shoulder, more than once he fell into stinging nettles, and one afternoon when winter had almost arrived, a horde of children hurled dirty snowballs at him. When a sheepdog bounded out of a wood, bit into his calf almost gently, and vanished again like a ghost, he decided this must stop. He was ill-suited to such dangers.

But he saw Johanna quite often now. It seemed as if she had always been somewhere nearby, only hidden from him by camouflage or lapses in his attention span. She walked ahead of him in the street, and it was as if his wish that she stop was enough to make her slow her step. Or she sat in church three rows behind him looking tired but concentrated as the pastor laid out their future damnation if they failed to make Christ's suffering their own, his cares their cares, his blood their blood; Gauss had long since given up wondering what this was supposed to mean, and was quite aware of how sarcastically she would look at him if he turned around now.

Once they went for a walk outside the town with her silly, perpetually sniggering friend Minna. They talked about new books he didn't know, how often it rained, the future of the Directory in Paris. Johanna often answered him before he'd finished speaking. He thought about seizing her and pulling her down onto the ground, and knew for sure that she could read his thoughts. Did they have to go through all this hypocrisy? Of course it was necessary, and when he accidentally touched her hand, he made a deep bow, as the nobility did, and she made a curtsey. On the way home he wondered if the day would ever come when people could deal with one another without lying. But before he could pursue that thought, he realized that every number could be expressed as the sum of three triangular numbers. Hands shaking, he groped for his pad, but he had left it at home by accident, and had to keep murmuring the formula softly to himself until they reached the next inn, where he tore a slate pencil out of the waiter's hand and scrawled it down on the tablecloth.

After that he never left his rooms. The days turned to evenings, the evenings to nights, which soaked up watery light in the early hours until day began again, all of it apparently as a matter of course. But it wasn't, death could arrive in a flash, he had to hurry. Sometimes Bartels came, bringing food. Sometimes his mother came. She stroked his head, looked at him with eyes swimming with love, and flushed with joy if he kissed her on the cheek. Then Zimmerman appeared, asked if he needed help with his work, saw his look, and went his way, mumbling in embarrassment. Letters from Lichtenberg, Büttner, and the secretary of the duke arrived; he didn't read any of them. Twice he had diarrhea, toothache three times, and one night such violent colic that he thought here it was, God wouldn't permit him to do this, the end was near. Another night, science, his work, his whole life all suddenly seemed strange and superfluous to him because he had no friend and no one apart from his mother to whom he meant anything. But that too passed, like everything else.

And then one rainy day, he was finished. He laid down his pen, blew his nose with extreme precision, and massaged his forehead. Already the memories of the last months, all the struggles, the decisions, the intellectual effort, were a thing of the past. They were the experiences of someone he suddenly no longer was. In front of him was the manuscript that this previous self had left behind, hundreds of tightly written pages. He leafed through it and asked himself how he could have pulled it off. He recalled no inspiration, no flashes of illumination. Just work.

The costs of having it printed meant he had to borrow from Bartels, who was almost penniless himself. Then there were problems when he insisted on reproofing the typeset pages personally; the idiot of a bookseller simply didn't understand that no one else was capable. Zimmerman wrote to the duke, who disgorged a little more money, and the *Disquisitiones*

Arithmeticae could appear. He had just turned twenty and his life's work was done. He knew: however long he remained on earth, he would never be able to achieve something comparable again.

He wrote a letter requesting Johanna's hand in marriage, and was refused. It was nothing to do with him personally, she wrote, it was just that she doubted anyone could exist side by side with him. She suspected he absorbed life and strength from the people around him the way the earth absorbed the sun or the sea absorbed the rivers, and that his company would condemn her to the pallid semi-unreality of a ghostly existence.

He nodded. He had expected this answer, if not its excellent underpinnings. Now only one thing remained.

The journey was a nightmare. His mother wept so copiously when they said goodbye that he might have been leaving for China, and then, although he had sworn he wouldn't, he wept too. The coach set off, and to begin with it was crammed with evil-smelling people; a woman ate raw eggs, shell and all, and a man kept up an uninterrupted stream of jokes that were blasphemous without being funny. Gauss tried to ignore it all by reading the latest issue of the *Monthly Correspondence Concerning the Advancement of Global and Celestial Knowledge*. The astronomer Piazzi's telescope had captured a ghost planet for several nights in a row, but before anyone could plot its course, it had vanished again. Perhaps an error, but then again perhaps a planetoid wandering between the inner and outer planets. But soon Gauss had to fold the newspaper away, as the sun was going down, the coach was jolting too much, and the egg-eating woman kept peeping over his shoulder. He closed his eyes. For a time he saw marching soldiers, then a firmament crisscrossed with magnetic lines, then Johanna, then he woke up. Rain was falling from a dull morning sky, but night was not over yet. The thought of more days and more nights, eleven and twenty-two respectively, beggared the imagination. Traveling was a horror!

When he reached Königsberg he was almost out of his mind with exhaustion, back pain, and boredom. He had no money for an inn, so he went straight to the university and got directions from a stupid-looking porter. Like everyone here, the man spoke a peculiar dialect, the streets looked foreign, the shops had signs that were incomprehensible, and the food in the taverns didn't smell like food. He had never been so far from home.

At last he found the address. He knocked; after a long wait a dust-enshrouded old man opened the door and, before Gauss could introduce himself, said the most gracious gentleman was not receiving visitors.

Gauss tried to explain who he was and where he'd come from.

The most gracious gentleman, the servant repeated, was not receiving. He himself had been working here longer than anyone would believe possible and he had never disobeyed an order.

Gauss pulled out letters of recommendation from Zimmerman, Kästner, Lichtenberg, and Pfaff. He insisted, said Gauss again. He could well imagine that there were a lot of visitors and that self-protection was necessary. But, and he must say this unequivocally, he was not just some nobody.

The servant had a think. His lips moved silently, and he didn't seem to know what to do next. Well, he murmured eventually, went inside, and left the door open.

Gauss followed him hesitantly down a short, dark hallway into a little room. It took a moment for his eyes to adjust to the half-light before he saw an ill-fitting window, a table, an armchair, and in it a motionless little dwarf wrapped in blankets: puffy lips, protruding forehead, thin, sharp nose. The eyes were half-open but didn't look at him. The air was so thick that it was almost impossible to breathe. Hoarsely he enquired if this might be the professor.

Who else, said the servant.

He moved over to the armchair and with trembling hands took out a copy of the *Disquisitiones*, on the flyleaf of which he had inscribed some words of veneration and thanks. He held out the book to the little man, but no hand lifted to take it. The servant instructed him in a whisper to put the book on the table.

In a hushed voice, he made his request: he had ideas he had never been able to share with anyone. For example, it seemed to him that Euclidean space did not, as per the *Critique of Pure Reason*, dictate the form of our perceptions and thus of all possible varieties of experience, but was, rather, a fiction, a beautiful dream. The truth was extremely strange: the proposition that two given parallel lines never touched each other had never been provable, not by Euclid, not by anyone else. But it wasn't at all obvious, as everyone had always assumed. He, Gauss, was thinking that the proposition was false. Perhaps there were no such things as parallels. Perhaps space also made it possible, provided one had a line and a point next to it, to draw infinite numbers of different parallels through this one point. Only one thing was certain: space was folded, bent, and extremely strange.

It felt good to utter all this out loud for the first time. The words were already coming faster, and his sentences were forming themselves of their own accord. This wasn't just some intellectual game! He maintained that . . . He was moving toward the window but a horrified squeak from the little man brought him to a halt. He maintained that a triangle of sufficient size, stretched between three stars out there, if measured exactly would have a different sum of its angles from the hundred-and-eighty-degree assumed total, and thus would prove itself to be a spherical body. When he looked up, gesticulating, he saw the cobwebs on the ceiling, in layers, all woven together into a kind of mat. One day it would be possible to achieve measurements like that! But that was a long way off, and meanwhile he needed the opinion of the only man who wouldn't think he was mad, and would definitely understand him. The man who had taught the world more about space and time than any other human being. He crouched down, so that his face was level with the little man's. He waited. The little eyes looked at him.

Sausage, said Kant.

Pardon?

Buy sausage, said Kant to the servant. And stars. Buy stars too.

Gauss stood up.

I have not lost all my manners, said Kant. Gentlemen! A drop of spittle ran down his cheek.

The gracious gentleman was tired, said the servant.

Gauss nodded. The servant stroked Kant's cheek with the back of his hand. The little man smiled weakly. They went out, the servant said goodbye with a silent bow. Gauss would gladly have given him some money, but he had none. At a distance he heard dark voices singing. The prison choir, said the servant. They'd always mightily disturbed the gracious gentleman.

In the coach, jammed in between a pastor and a fat lieutenant who tried desperately to draw his fellow travelers into conversation, he read the article about the mysterious planet for the third time. Of course you could calculate its course! All you had to do was start from an ellipse rather than a circle when making your approximations and then go about it more skillfully than these idiots had done. A few days' work and you'd be able to predict when or where it would appear again. When the lieutenant asked his opinion about the Franco-Spanish alliance, he didn't know what to say.

Didn't he think, asked the lieutenant, it would be the end of Austria?

He shrugged his shoulders.

And this Bonaparte person?

I'm sorry, who? he asked.

Back in Brunswick he wrote another proposal to Johanna. Then he fetched the little bottle of curare from the poison cupboard at the Institute of Chemistry. Some researcher had recently sent it across the ocean along with a collection of plants, stones, and papers crammed with notes, a chemist had brought it here from Berlin, since when it had just been standing there, and nobody knew what to do with it. Apparently even a tiny dose was deadly. They would tell his mother he had had a heart attack, without any warning, nothing to be done, God's will. He summoned a messenger from the street, sealed the letter, and paid for it with his last coins. Then he stared out of the window and waited.

He uncorked the flask. The liquid had no smell. Would he hesitate? Probably. It was the kind of thing you didn't know before you really tried it. But he was surprised to feel so little fear. The messenger would bring her refusal and then his death would be no more than a move in a chess game, something heaven hadn't reckoned on. He had been sent into the world with an intellect that rendered almost everything human impossible, in a time when every task was hard, exhausting, and dirty. God had tried to make fun of him.

And the other possibility, now that the work had been written? Years of mediocrity, earning one's bread in some degrading fashion, compromises, fear and vexation, more compromises, physical and spiritual pain, and the slow erosion of all faculties on the way to the feebleness of old age. No!

With astonishing clarity he became aware how violently he was trembling. He heard the roaring in his ears, observed the twitching in his hands, listened to his breath as it came in short gasps. He could almost find it funny.

A knock at the door. A voice, vaguely like his own, called, Come in!

The messenger came, pressed a piece of paper into his hand, and waited with an impertinent look for a tip. He found one more coin at the bottom of the bottommost drawer. The messenger threw it into the air, made a half turn, and caught it behind his back. Seconds later, he saw him running down the alley.

He thought about the Last Judgment. He didn't believe any such event would happen. Those accused could defend themselves, and many questions posed in rebuttal would make God quite uncomfortable. Insects. Dirt. Pain. The inadequacy of everything. Even time and space had been bungled. If he found himself before such a court, he would have a few things to say.

His hands numb, he opened Johanna's letter, laid it aside, and reached for the little flask. Suddenly he had the feeling that there was something he had overlooked. He thought. Something unexpected had happened. He closed the bottle, thought harder, still couldn't work out what it was. Then suddenly it dawned on him that what he had read was her acceptance.

The River

The days in Caracas passed swiftly. They had to climb Silla without a guide, because it turned out that not a single native had even set foot on the twin peaks. Bonpland's nose soon wouldn't stop bleeding, and their most expensive barometer fell down and broke. Near the summit they found petrified mussels. Strange, said Humboldt, the water could never have been that high, so it must indicate an upward folding of the earth's crust, i.e., forces from its interior.

Up on the peak, they were persecuted by a swarm of furry bees. Bonpland threw himself flat on the ground, while Humboldt remained upright, sextant in hand and the eyepiece against his insect-covered face. They were crawling over his forehead, his nose, his chin, and down inside his collar. The governor had warned him that the most important thing was not to touch them. Or breathe. Just wait them out.

Bonpland asked if he could lift his head again.

Better not, said Humboldt without moving his lips. After a quarter of an hour, the creatures detached themselves and whirred off in a dark cloud into the sunset. Humboldt admitted it hadn't been easy to hold still. Once or twice he had been close to screaming. He sat down and rubbed his forehead. His nerves were not what they had been.

To bid them farewell there was an open-air concert in the Caracas theater. Gluck's chords rose into the darkness, the night was huge and full of stars, and Bonpland had tears in his eyes. He didn't really know, whispered Humboldt, music had never said very much to him.

They set off toward the Orinoco with a train of mules. Around the capital the plains stretched away unbroken for thousands of miles, without a tree or bush or hill. It was so bright that they had the sense they were walking on a glistening mirror, with their shadows below them and the empty sky above, or that they were reflections of two creatures from another world. At some point Bonpland asked if they were still alive.

He didn't know either, said Humboldt, but one way or the other, what could they do except keep going?

When they first caught sight of trees, swamps, and grass again, they had no idea how long they had been traveling. Humboldt had difficulty reading his two chronometers, he had lost any sense of time. Huts appeared, people came to meet them, and only when he had asked several times about what day it was did they believe they had been walking for no more than two weeks.

In Calabozo they met an old man who had never left his village. In spite of this he possessed a laboratory: glass vessels and bottles, metal equipment for measuring earthquakes, humidity, and magnetism. Plus

95

a primitive machine with pointers that moved if anyone in the vicinity told a lie or said something stupid. And an apparatus which clicked and hummed and made sparks fly between dozens of little wheels rotating against each other. He was the one who had discovered this mysterious power, the old man cried. That proved he was a great scientist!

Doubtless, replied Humboldt, but —

Bonpland poked him in the side. The old man cranked harder, the sparks crackled louder and louder, the voltage was so strong that their hair was standing on end.

Impressive, said Humboldt, but the phenomenon was called galvanism and was known around the world. He too had something with him that produced the same effects, but much stronger. He showed the Leyden jar and how rubbing it with a hide would produce the tiniest branching flashes of lightning.

The old man scratched his chin in silence.

Humboldt clapped him on the shoulder and wished him all the luck in the future. Bonpland wanted to give the old man money, but he wouldn't take any.

He couldn't have known, he said. They were so far from anywhere.

Of course, said Bonpland.

The old man blew his nose and repeated that he couldn't have known. Until they were out of sight, they saw him standing bent over in front of his house, looking after them.

They came to a pond. Bonpland pulled off his clothes, climbed in, stopped for a moment, groaned, and then sank his full length. The water was full of electric eels.

Three days later Humboldt wrote down the results of their investigation with a numb hand. The animals could deliver shocks without even being touched. The shock produced no sparks, no reaction on the electrometer, no deviation of the magnetic needle; in short it left no trace except the pain it delivered. If one seized the eel in both hands or held it in one hand while holding a piece of metal in the other, the effect was stronger. It was the same if two people held hands and only one of them touched the animal. In this case both felt the shock at the same moment and with the same force. Only the front of the eel was dangerous, eels themselves were immune to their own discharges. And the pain itself was immense; so strong that it was impossible to tell what was happening. It expressed itself in numbness, confusion, and dizziness, only afterwards was it recognizable, and it continued to grow in memory; it seemed more like something that belonged to the outside world than to one's own body.

Satisfied, they continued their journey. What a stroke of luck, said Humboldt again and again, what a gift! Bonpland was limping, and there was no feeling in his hands. Days later, sparks were still dancing across Humboldt's field of vision when he closed his eyes. For a long time his knees were as stiff as an old man's.

In the high grass they came upon an unconscious girl, maybe thirteen years old, in torn clothes. Bonpland dripped medicine into her mouth, she spat, coughed, and then began to scream. While he talked at her soothingly, Humboldt walked impatiently up and down. Rigid with fear she looked from one to the other. Bonpland stroked her head, and she began to sob. Someone must have done something appalling to her, he said.

What, asked Humboldt.

Bonpland gave him a long look.

Well, whatever it was, said Humboldt, they had to get on.

Bonpland gave her water, which she drank hastily. She wouldn't eat. He helped her to her feet. Without a sign of gratitude she pulled herself free and ran away.

Must have been the heat, said Humboldt. Children got lost and passed out.

Bonpland stared at him for a while. Yes, he said. Probably.

In the town of San Fernando they sold their mules and bought a wide sailboat with a wooden superstructure on the deck, provisions for a month, and reliable weapons. Humboldt made enquiries about anyone who might be familiar with the river. He was directed to four men seated in front of a tavern. One of them was wearing a top hat, one of them had a reed sticking out of the corner of his mouth, one of them was festooned with brass jewelry, and the fourth was pale and arrogant and didn't utter a word.

Humboldt asked if they might know the channel that ran between the Orinoco and the Amazon.

Of course, said the man with the top hat.

He had already traveled it, said the man with the jewelry.

Him too, said the man with the top hat. But it didn't exist. All a rumor.

Humboldt, confused, said nothing. Well anyway, was his final remark, he wanted to measure this channel, and he would need experienced oarsmen.

The man with the top hat asked what the prize was. Money and knowledge.

The third man used two fingers to remove the reed from his mouth. Money, he said, was better than knowledge.

Much better, said the man with the top hat. And besides, life was so damn short, why gamble on it?

Because it was short, said Bonpland.

The four of them looked at one another, then at Humboldt. Their names, said the man with the top hat, were Carlos, Gabriel, Mario, and Julio, and they were good but they weren't cheap.

That was all right, said Humboldt.

He was followed to the inn by a rough sheepdog. When Humboldt stood still, the dog came up and pressed its nose against his shoe. When Humboldt scratched him behind the ears, he hiccuped, then whimpered with pleasure, fell back, and growled at Bonpland.

He liked him, said Humboldt. Obviously he had no master, so he'd take him along.

The boat was too small, said Bonpland. The dog was rabid and smelled bad.

They would soon get on with each other, said Humboldt, and let the dog sleep in his room at the inn. When the two of them arrived at the boat the following morning, they were as easy with each other as if they'd always been together.

Nobody had said anything about dogs, said Julio.

Further south, said Mario as he straightened his top hat, where the people were mad and talked backwards, there were dwarf dogs with wings. He had seen them himself.

Him too, said Julio. But now they'd died out. Eaten by the talking fish.

With a sigh, Humboldt used sextant and chronometer to determine the position of the town; once again the maps had been inaccurate. Then they cast off.

Soon all traces of the settlement were left behind. They saw crocodiles everywhere: the animals were floating in the water like tree trunks, dozing on the bank or gaping their jaws wide, and on their backs little herons walked around. The dog jumped into the water. A crocodile swam at him immediately, and as Bonpland pulled him back on board, his paw was bleeding from a piranha bite. Lianas brushed the surface of the water and tree trunks leaned out over the river.

They moored the boat and while Bonpland gathered plants, Humboldt went for a walk. He clambered over roots, squeezed a way between tree trunks, and brushed the threads of a spider's web out of his face. He detached flowers from stalks, broke the back of a beautiful butterfly with a skilled hand, and laid it lovingly in his specimen box. Only then did he notice that he was standing in front of a jaguar.

The animal raised its head and looked at him. Humboldt took a step to the side. Without stirring, the

100

animal lifted its lip. Humboldt froze. After a long time it laid its head down on its forepaws. Humboldt took a step back. And another. The jaguar watched him attentively, without raising its head. Its tail switched in pursuit of a fly. Humboldt turned. He listened, but he heard nothing behind him. Holding his breath, arms pressed tight against his body, head down on his chest, and his eyes fixed on his feet, he began to move. Slowly, step by step, then gradually quicker. He must not stumble, he must not look back. And then he couldn't help himself, he began to run. Branches reared into his face, an insect smacked against his forehead, he slipped, grabbed hold of a liana, one sleeve got caught and tore, he struck branches out of his way. Sweating and out of breath, he reached the boat.

Cast off immediately, he panted.

Bonpland reached for his gun, the oarsmen got to their feet.

No, said Humboldt, cast off!

These were good weapons, said Bonpland. They could kill the animal and it would make a wonderful trophy.

Humboldt shook his head.

But why not?

The jaguar had let him go.

Bonpland muttered something about superstition and untied the ropes. The oarsmen grinned. Once in the middle of the current, Humboldt could no longer understand his own fear. He decided to describe events in his diary the way they should have happened: he would claim they had gone back into the undergrowth, guns cocked, but had failed to find the animal.

Before he had finished his account, the skies opened. The boat filled with water and they steered hastily for dry land. They reached it to be greeted by a naked, bearded man so covered in filth as to be almost unrecognizable. This was his plantation, for a fee they could spend the night.

Humboldt paid and asked where the house was.

He didn't have one, said the man. He was Don Ignacio, he was a Castilian nobleman, and the whole world was his house. And these were his wife and daughter.

Humboldt bowed to the two naked women and didn't know where to look. The oarsmen attached expanses of fabric to the trees and cowered down underneath them.

Don Ignacio asked if there was anything else they needed.

Not at the moment, said Humboldt, exhausted.

None of his guests, said Don Ignacio, would ever suffer want. With dignity he turned on his heel and walked away. Raindrops pearled on his head and shoulders. It smelled of flowers, wet earth, and manure.

Sometimes, said Bonpland reflectively, it struck him as an absolute enigma that he was here. Indescribably far from home, dispatched by nobody's ruler, simply because of a Prussian he'd met on the stairs.

Humboldt lay awake for a long time. The oarsmen kept on whispering wild stories to one another which lodged in his brain. And every time he managed to banish the flying houses, threatening serpent women, and fights to the death, he saw the eyes of the jaguar. Alert, intelligent, and pitiless. Then he came to again and heard the rain, the men, and the dog growling anxiously. At some point Bonpland arrived, wrapped himself in his blanket, and immediately went to sleep. Humboldt hadn't even heard him leave.

Next morning, with the sun high in the sky, it was as if it had never rained, and Don Ignacio said farewell to them with the gestures of a chatelain. They would always be welcome here! His wife gave a perfect court curtsey, and his daughter stroked Bonpland's arm. He put his hand on her shoulder and pulled a strand of hair off her face.

The wind was as hot as if it were coming out of an oven. The growth on the banks was getting thicker. White turtles' eggs lay under the trees, lizards clung like wooden ornaments to the hull of the boat. Reflections of birds kept moving over the water, even when the sky was empty.

Remarkable optical phenomenon, said Humboldt.

Optical had nothing to do with it, said Mario. Birds were constantly dying at every moment, in fact they did little else. Their spirits lived on in their reflections. They had to go somewhere and they weren't wanted in heaven.

And insects, asked Bonpland.

They didn't die at all. That was the problem.

And indeed, the mosquitoes came interminably. They came out of the trees, the air, the water, they came from all sides, filling the air with their whining, stinging,

103

sucking, and for every one that got squashed, there were a hundred more. Not even thick clothes thrown over their heads brought any relief, the creatures just stung right through the material.

The river, said Julio, didn't tolerate anyone. Before Aguirre had come this way, he had been sane. Only once he got here did he have the idea of declaring himself emperor.

A madman and a murderer, said Bonpland, the first explorer of the Orinoco. That made sense!

This sad man didn't explore a thing, said Humboldt. Any more than a bird explores the air or a fish explores water.

Or a German explores humor, said Bonpland.

Humboldt looked at him with a frown.

Just a joke, said Bonpland.

But an unfair one. Prussians could laugh. People laughed a lot in Prussia. Just think of Wieland's novels or those outstanding comedies of Gryphius. Even Herder knew how to set up a good joke.

He was sure, said Bonpland wearily.

Then that was all right, said Humboldt, scratching the dog's insect-bitten and bleeding coat.

They started up the Orinoco. The river was so wide that it was like sailing on the sea: far in the distance, like a mirage, forests showed on the other bank. Now there were hardly any waterbirds. The sky seemed to shimmer in the heat.

After some hours, Humboldt discovered that fleas had buried themselves in the skin of his toes. They had to interrupt their journey; Bonpland classified plants,

Humboldt sat in a camp chair, his feet in a bucket of vinegar, and mapped the course of the river. *Pulex penetrans*, the common sand flea. He would describe it, but nowhere in his diary was he going to mention that he himself had fallen victim to it.

It's not that bad, said Bonpland.

Humboldt said he'd thought a lot about the rules of fame. If it was known that a man had had fleas living underneath his toenails, nobody would take him seriously. No matter what his achievements had been.

Next day they had a mishap. They had reached a particular broad expanse where both banks were invisible when the wind reversed the sail against the direction of the boat, the boat dipped, a wave slopped in, and dozens of pieces of paper were floating away in the water. The boat tilted further, the water reached their knees, the dog howled, and the men wanted to jump overboard. Humboldt leapt up; in a flash he loosened the belt with the chronometer and barked in an officer's voice that nobody was to move. The current let the boat drift, the sail flopped uselessly to and fro, and the gray backs of several crocodiles came closer.

Bonpland volunteered to swim to shore and get help.

There was no help, said Humboldt, holding the belt up over his head. In case no one had noticed, this was primeval forest. The only thing to do was wait.

It was true: at the last moment the sail caught the wind and the boat slowly righted itself.

Bail the boat, yelled Humboldt.

The oarsmen cursed one another and went to work with pots, caps, and drinking mugs. In short order, the

105

boat was back on an even keel. Pieces of paper, dried plants, quill pens, and books were all swimming in the river. Off in the distance a top hat seemed to be hurrying to escape.

Sometimes he despaired, said Bonpland, that he would ever get home.

That was just being realistic, replied Humboldt, checking to see if any of the timepieces were damaged.

They came to the infamous cataracts. The river was full of rocks and the water bubbled as if it were boiling. It was impossible to advance any further with the laden boat. There was a mission there, and the Jesuits, heavily armed and stocky, more like soldiers than priests, received them mistrustfully. Humboldt sought out the head of the mission, a lean man with a fever-jaundiced face, and showed him his passport.

Good, said Pater Zea. He called an order through the window and shortly thereafter six monks brought in two natives. These excellent men, said Pater Zea, who would know the cataracts better than anyone, had volunteered of their own accord to bring a suitable boat through the rapids. Please would the guests wait until the boat was ready further down, then they could continue their journey. He made a gesture; his people led the two natives out and shackled their ankles.

He was most grateful, said Humboldt carefully, but he couldn't allow it.

Oh nonsense, cried Pater Zea, it didn't mean a thing, it was just because these people were erratic. They volunteered themselves and then all of a sudden they were nowhere to be found. And they all looked alike!

The boat for the next stage of their journey was brought. It was so narrow that they would have to sit one behind the other on the chests that held their instruments.

Better a month in hell than this, said Bonpland.

He would have both, promised Pater Zea. Hell and the boat.

In the evening they were served the first good dinner in weeks, and even Spanish wine. Through the window they could hear the oarsmen interrupting one another as they argued about the proper outcome of a story.

He had the impression, said Humboldt, that storytelling went on here all the time. What was the point of this eternal singsong recital of totally invented lives, which didn't even have a moral in them?

They had tried everything, said Pater Zea. All colonies banned the writing down of made-up stories. But people were stubborn and even the holy power of the Church had its limits. It was something to do with the country. He wondered if the baron had met the famous La Condamine.

Humboldt shook his head.

But he had, said Bonpland. An old man who fought with the waiters in the Palais Royal.

That was him, said the pater. There were one or two old men around here who remembered him. And a woman, who went into a decline as the result of some powder from a bad medicine man, but couldn't die, a horrible sight, he might add. Their stories were worth hearing. Might he tell them?

Humboldt sighed.

Back then, said Pater Zea, the Academy had sent out their three best surveyors, La Condamine, Bouguer, and Godin, to establish the length of the meridian of the equator. The hope had been, if only on aesthetic grounds, to disprove Newton's ugly theory that the earth was flattening itself by its own rotation. Pater Zea stared fixedly at the table for a few seconds. An enormous insect landed on his forehead. Instinctively Bonpland reached out his hand, stopped, and then pulled it back again.

To measure the equator, Pater Zea continued. In other words to draw a line where no line had been before. Had they looked around outside? Lines happened somewhere else. His bony arm pointed to the window, the bushes, the plants covered in swarms of insects. Not here!

Lines happened everywhere, said Humboldt. They were an abstraction. Wherever there was space as such, there were lines.

Space as such was elsewhere, said Pater Zea.

Space was universal!

Being universal was an invention. And space as such happened where surveyors put it. Pater Zea closed his eyes, lifted his wineglass, and set it down again without drinking from it. The three men had worked with extraordinary precision. Nonetheless, their data never matched. Point zero two degrees of angle on La Condamine's instrument was point zero three on Bouguer's, and half a degree in Godin's telescope was one and a half in La Condamine's. In order to draw their line, they were advised to use astronomical measurements, since practical, portable clocks like this, and here he eyed the chronometer on Humboldt's belt with a mocking glance, didn't yet exist. Things weren't yet used to being measured. Three stones and three leaves were not yet the same number, fifteen grams of peas and fifteen grams of earth not yet the same weight. Then add the heat, the damp, the mosquitoes, the never-ending noises of animals fighting. An unfathomable, pointless rage had overcome the men. The perfectly mannered La Condamine had misplaced Bouguer's measuring instruments, Bouguer in turn had broken Godin's pencils. There were daily battles, until Godin drew his sword and staggered away into the primeval forest. Two weeks later, the same thing happened between Bouguer and La Condamine. Pater Zea folded his hands. Imagine! Such civilized men, with full perukes, lorgnons, and scented handkerchiefs! La Condamine held out the longest. Eight years in the forest, protected by a mere handful of fever-ridden soldiers. He had cut trails which grew back again as soon as he turned his back, felled trees which resprouted the next night, and yet, little by little, with stiff-necked determination, he had forcibly imposed a web of numbers over reluctant nature. He had drawn triangles which gradually approximated a sum of a hundred and eighty degrees and triangulated arcs whose curves finally stood strong even in the shimmering heat. Then he received a letter from the Academy. The battle was lost, the proof followed Newton, the earth was indeed oblate, all his work had been in vain.

Bonpland took a large mouthful from the wine bottle. He seemed to have forgotten that there were wineglasses and that this wasn't done. Humboldt punished him with a glare.

And so, said Pater Zea, the beaten man went home. Four months to travel down a still-nameless river, which he only later christened the Amazon. On the way he painted maps, gave mountains names, tracked the temperature, and worked out the species of fishes, insects, snakes, and humans. Not because it interested him, but in order to stay sane. Afterwards, back in Paris, he never talked about the things that one or another of his soldiers remembered: the throaty sounds and perfectly aimed poisoned arrows that came flying out of the undergrowth, the nocturnal glows, but above all the minuscule displacements of reality, when the world crossed over into otherworldliness for a few moments. At such times the trees looked like trees and the slowly swirling water looked like water, but it was mimicry, it was something foreign, and it caused a shudder. It was at this time that La Condamine also found the channel that mad Aguirre had spoken of. The channel connecting the two greatest rivers on the continent.

He would prove its existence, said Humboldt. All great rivers were connected. Nature was a unity.

Oh yes? Pater Zea shook his head skeptically. Years later, when La Condamine, long since a member of the Academy and old and famous, was able (mostly) to wake from sleep without screaming and once again to make himself believe in God, he declared the channel to be an error. Great rivers, he said, had no inland connection. Such a thing would be a disorder of nature, and unworthy of a great continent. Pater Zea fell silent for a moment, then got to his feet and bowed. Dream well, Baron, and wake in good health!

Early next morning they were jolted from sleep by howls of pain. One of the men chained up in the courtyard was being beaten with leather whips by two priests. Humboldt ran out and asked what was going on.

Nothing, said one of the priests. Why?

A very old affair, said the other. It had nothing to do with their onward journey. He kicked the Indian, who took a minute to understand before summoning his bad Spanish to say that it was a very old affair and had nothing to do with their journey.

Humboldt hesitated. Bonpland, who had joined him, looked at him reproachfully. But they had to move on, Humboldt said quietly. What was he supposed to do?

Pater Zea called to them to come, so that he could show them his most priceless possession. A moth-eaten parrot, who could say several sentences in an extinct language. Twenty years ago the people who spoke it had still existed, but they had all died out and nobody could understand what the bird was gabbling.

Humboldt stretched out his hand, the parrot pecked at it, looked at the ground as if thinking, flapped its wings, and said something incomprehensible.

Bonpland enquired why the tribe had disappeared.

It happened, said Pater Zea.

Why?

Pater Zea stared at him with narrowed eyes. It was easy to be like that. A person came here and pitied anyone who looked sad, and back home there would be bad stories to tell, but if that person suddenly found himself with fifty men ruling ten thousand savages, wondering every night what the voices in the forest meant, and being amazed each morning to find himself alive, perhaps he would judge things differently.

A misunderstanding, said Humboldt. Nobody had intended to criticize.

Well, yes, maybe he had, said Bonpland. There were some things he wanted to know. He stopped, unable to believe that Humboldt had just kicked him. The bird swiveled its head between them, said something, then looked at them expectantly.

Correct, replied Humboldt, who didn't want to be impolite.

The bird seemed to think about this, then added a long sentence.

Humboldt stretched out his hand, the bird jabbed at it, and turned away, insulted.

While the two Indians were navigating the boat through the cataracts for them, Humboldt and Bonpland climbed the granite cliffs above the mission. There was supposed to be an ancient burial cave at the top. It was almost impossible to find a foothold, the only supports were protruding crystals of feldspar. Once they were up there, Humboldt put pen to paper to compose a piece of perfect prose describing the view of the rapids, the rainbow soaring over the river, and the watery glints of silver in the distance. The only thing to break his concentration was the need to keep slapping at mosquitoes. Then they balanced their way across the ridge to the next peak and the entrance to the cave.

There must have been hundreds of corpses, each in its own basket of palm leaves, the bony hands clasped around the knees, the head pressed down against the chest cavity. The oldest were already reduced to skeletons, others were in varying states of decay: parchment scraps of skin, intestines dried in clumps, eyes black and small as fruit kernels. Lots of them had the flesh scratched from the bones. The noise of the river didn't penetrate this high; it was so quiet they could hear their own breathing.

It was peaceful here, said Bonpland, nothing like that other cave. Down there had been the dead, here there were just bodies. Here it felt safe.

Humboldt tugged several corpses out of their baskets, detached skulls from spines, broke teeth out of jawbones and rings from fingers. He wrapped the bodies of a child and two adults in cloths and tied them together so tightly that two people could carry the bundle.

Bonpland asked if he was serious.

He should grab hold right now, said Humboldt impatiently, he couldn't get them down to the mules on his own!

It was late before they reached the mission. The night was clear, the stars particularly bright, insect swarms tinged the light red, and the air smelled of vanilla. The Indians backed silently away from them. Old women stared out of windows, children fled. A man with a painted face stepped into their path and asked what was in the cloths.

Various things, said Humboldt. This and that.

Rock samples, said Bonpland. Plants.

The man folded his arms.

Bones, said Humboldt.

Bones?

Of crocodiles and sea cows, said Bonpland.

Sea cows, the man said after him.

Humboldt asked if he'd like to see them.

Better not. The man stepped slowly aside. Better to believe him.

The next two days did not go well. They couldn't find any Indian guides who were prepared to show them the area, and even the Jesuits were in a hurry when Humboldt spoke to them. These people were all so superstitious, he wrote to his brother, that it was going to be a long time yet before they attained freedom and reason. But at least he'd managed to capture a few little monkeys unknown to biologists so far.

On the third day the two volunteers brought the boat unscathed through the rapids with only minor injuries to themselves. Humboldt gave them some money and a few glass marbles, had the cases of instruments, the caged monkeys, and the corpses loaded on board, and assured Pater Zea of his lifelong gratitude as he said goodbye.

He should take care, said the pater, or it would be a short one.

The four oarsmen arrived and there was a vigorous discussion about loading. First the dog, then that! Julio pointed to the cloth bundle with the corpses.

Humboldt asked if they were afraid.

Of course, said Mario.

But of what, said Bonpland. That the bodies were suddenly going to wake up?

Exactly, said Julio.

Anyhow, it was going to cost them, said Carlos.

Above the cataracts, the river was very narrow, and rapids kept hurling the boat from side to side. Spray saturated the air and they had to move dangerously close to the cliffs. The mosquitoes were relentless: the sky seemed to be entirely composed of insects. The men soon gave up swatting at them. They had got used to the fact that they were constantly bleeding.

At the next mission they were given ant paste to eat. Bonpland refused it, but Humboldt tasted a mouthful. Then he excused himself and disappeared into the undergrowth for some time. Not uninteresting, he said, when he came back. Certainly a possible future solution to the food supply.

But this place was completely uninhabited, said Bonpland. The only thing in full supply was food!

The village chief asked what was in the cloth bundles. He had a terrible suspicion.

Sea cow bones, said Bonpland.

That was not what it smelled of, said the chief.

Very well, cried Humboldt, he would admit it. But these dead were so old, they couldn't even be described as corpses any more. In the final analysis, the entire world was made up of dead bodies! Every handful of earth had once been a person and another person before that, and every ounce of air had already been breathed by thousands and thousands now dead. What was the matter with them all, what was the problem?

He had only asked, said the chief shyly.

To ward off mosquitoes, the villagers had built mud huts with entrances that could be closed. They lit fires inside to drive out the insects, then crawled in and blocked the entrance, put out the fire, and were able to spend a few hours in the hot air without being bitten. In one of these huts Bonpland spent so much time cataloguing the plants they had gathered that he fainted from the smoke. Humboldt sat in the next hut coughing and half-blind, with the dog, writing to his brother. When they emerged, with stinking clothes, gasping for air, a man came running up to them, wanting to read their palms. He was naked, with brightly colored body paint and feathers in his hair. Humboldt refused, but Bonpland was interested. The soothsayer took hold of his fingers, raised his eyebrows, and looked in amusement at his hand.

Ah, he said, as if to himself. Ah, ah.

Yes?

The soothsayer shook his head. He was sure it was nothing. Things could happen one way or the other. Everyone forged his own luck. Who could know the future!

Nervously, Bonpland asked what he saw.

Long life. The soothsayer shrugged. No doubt about it.

And health?

Generally good.

Dammit, cried Bonpland. Now he demanded to know what that look had meant.

What look? Long life and health. That's what was there, that's what he said. Did the gentleman like this continent?

Why?

He was going to be here for a very long time.

Bonpland laughed. He doubted it. A long life, here of all places? Certainly not. Unless someone forced him.

The soothsayer sighed and held his hand for a moment, as if to give him courage. Then he turned to Humboldt.

Who shook his head.

It hardly cost a thing!

No, said Humboldt.

In one swift movement, the soothsayer grabbed Humboldt's hand. He tried to pull away but the soothsayer was stronger; Humboldt, forced to play along, gave a sour smile. The soothsayer frowned and pulled the hand closer. He bent forward, then straightened up again. Squeezed his eyes together. Puffed out his cheeks.

Just say it, cried Humboldt. He had other things to do. If something bad was there, it didn't matter, he didn't believe a word of it anyway.

Nothing bad there.

But?

Nothing. The soothsayer let go of Humboldt's hand. He was sorry, he didn't want any money, he couldn't do it.

He didn't understand, said Humboldt.

Him neither. It was nothing. No past, no present, no future. There was, so to speak, nothing and nobody to see. The soothsayer looked sharply into Humboldt's face. Nobody!

Humboldt stared at his hand.

Of course it was nonsense. Of course it was the man's fault. Perhaps he was losing his gift. The soothsayer squashed a gnat on his belly. Perhaps he'd never had it.

That evening, Humboldt and Bonpland left the dog tied up next to the oarsmen, so that they could have an insect-free night in the smoke-huts. It wasn't until the early hours of the morning that Humboldt nodded off to sleep, soaked with sweat, eyes burning, his thoughts a blur in the fug.

He was awakened by a noise. Someone had crawled in and was lying down beside him. Not again, he muttered, lit the candle stub with shaky fingers, and found himself looking at a small boy. What do you want, he asked, what's the matter, what is this all about?

The child examined him with little animal eyes.

So what is it, asked Humboldt, what?

The boy kept staring at him. He was completely naked. In spite of the flame in front of his eyes, he didn't blink.

What, whispered Humboldt, what, child?

118

The boy laughed.

Humboldt's hand was shaking so badly that he dropped the candle. In the darkness he could hear them both breathing. He reached out his hand to push the boy away, but when he felt his damp skin, he recoiled as if he'd been hit. Go away, he whispered.

The boy didn't move.

Humboldt sprang to his feet, bumping his head on the roof, and kicked at him. The boy screamed — since the business with the sand fleas Humboldt wore boots at night — and rolled himself into a ball. Humboldt kicked again and hit the boy's head, the boy whimpered softly and then went quiet. Humboldt could hear himself panting. He saw the shadowy body in front of him, seized him by the shoulders, and pushed him out.

The night air did him good; after the thick fug in the hut it felt cool and fresh. Walking unsteadily, he went to the next hut, where Bonpland was. But when he heard a woman's voice, he stopped. He listened, and heard it again. He turned back, crawled into his hut, and closed the entrance. The curtain had been open for long enough to let the insects fly in, and a panicked bat fluttered round his head. My God, he whispered. Then, out of sheer exhaustion, he fell into a restless sleep.

When he woke up, it was broad daylight, the heat was even more intense, and the bat was gone. Impeccably dressed, his uniform dagger at his side, and his hat under his arm, he stepped out into the open air. The area in front of the huts was empty. His face was bleeding from several cuts.

Bonpland asked what had happened to him.

He had tried to shave himself. Just because there were mosquitoes was no reason to turn savage, one was still a civilized human being. Humboldt set his hat on his head and asked if Bonpland had heard anything during the night.

Nothing special, said Bonpland carefully. One heard all sorts of things in the night.

Humboldt nodded. And one dreamed the strangest dreams.

Next day they turned in to the Rio Negro, where the mosquitoes were less plentiful over the dark water. The air too was better here. But the presence of the corpses was weighing on the oarsmen, and even Humboldt was pale and silent. Bonpland kept his eyes closed. He was afraid, he said, that his fever was coming back. The monkeys screamed in their cages, rattled the bars, and pulled faces at one another. One of them even managed to open its door, turned somersaults, plagued the oarsmen, went climbing along the edge of the boat, jumped onto Humboldt's shoulders, and spat at the snarling dog.

Mario asked Humboldt if he would please tell them a story.

He didn't know any stories, said Humboldt, as he straightened his hat, which the monkey had turned around. And he didn't like telling them. But he could recite the most beautiful poem in the German language, freely translated into Spanish. Here it was. Above all the mountaintops it was silent, there was no wind in the trees, even the birds were quiet, and soon death would come.[1]

Everyone looked at him.

That's it, said Humboldt.

Yes, but, asked Bonpland.

Humboldt reached for the sextant.

Pardon, said Julio, but that couldn't have been the whole thing.

Of course it wasn't some story about blood, war, and shape-changing, snapped Humboldt. There was no act of magic in it, nobody got turned into a plant or began to fly or ate somebody else. With one swift grab he seized the monkey who was just in the process of trying to undo his shoes, and stuck him in his cage. The little creature screamed, tried to bite him, stuck out its tongue, moved its ears, and showed him its backside. And unless he was mistaken, said Humboldt, everyone on this boat had work to do!

Near San Carlos they crossed the magnetic equator. Humboldt watched the instruments devoutly. He had dreamed of this place when he was a child.

It was almost evening when they reached the mouth of the legendary channel. Swarms of biting flies immediately descended on them. But as the heat dissipated, so did the haze; the sky cleared, and Humboldt could measure the degree of longitude. He worked all night, measuring the angle of the moon as it

---

[1] *Translator's note:* Alert readers will recognize this as a scientist's prosaically exact rendition of Goethe's 'Wanderer's Nightsong.' It must be said that Goethe did it better.

tracked across the Southern Cross. Then, by way of confirmation, fixing the ghostly spots of Jupiter's moons in his telescope. Nothing could be relied on, he said to the dog, who was observing him intently. Not the tables, not the instruments, not even the sky. One had to be so precise as to be immune to disorder.

It was almost dawn when he finished. He clapped his hands, get up everybody, no time to lose! One end of the channel was now pinpointed, and they had to reach the other as quickly as possible.

Sleepily Bonpland asked if he was afraid someone might beat him to it, given that it was at the end of the world, and entire centuries had passed without the goddamn river attracting the slightest attention.

One never knew, said Humboldt.

The region had never been mapped, and they could only guess where the water was carrying them. Tree trunks crowded the bank so tightly that it was impossible to land, and every few hours a thin spray of rain would moisten the air without cooling it or discouraging the insects. Bonpland made a whistling sound whenever he breathed.

It was nothing, he said, coughing, it was just that he didn't know whether it was the fever or something in the air. Speaking as a doctor, he suggested it wasn't a good idea to inhale too deeply. He suspected the woods were giving off unhealthy vapors. Or maybe it was the corpses.

Out of the question, said Humboldt. The corpses had nothing to do with it.

Eventually they found a place to land, and took machetes and axes to chop out a small space where they could spend the night. Mosquitoes crepitated in the flames of their campfire. A bat bit the dog in the nose; he bled profusely, turned circles growling, and wouldn't settle down again. He went to hide under Humboldt's hammock, and his rumbling kept them awake for a long time.

Next morning neither Humboldt nor Bonpland was able to shave: their faces were too swollen from insect bites. When they went to cool their swelling in the river, they realized that the dog was missing. Humboldt quickly loaded his gun.

Not a good idea, said Carlos. The forest was at its thickest, and the air was too wet for guns. The dog must have been taken by a jaguar; nothing to be done.

Without saying a word, Humboldt disappeared into the trees.

Nine hours later they were still there. The seventeenth time Humboldt came back, drank water, washed himself in the river, and tried to set off again, Bonpland held him back.

There was no point, the dog was gone.

Never. Absolutely not, said Humboldt. He wouldn't permit it.

Bonpland put a hand on his shoulder. The dog was damn well dead!

As a doornail, said Julio.

Gone for good, said Mario.

It was certainly the deadest dog in history, said Carlos.

123

Humboldt looked at them all, one after the other. His mouth opened and closed, but then he laid down the gun.

It was days before they saw another settlement. A missionary turned half-witted by the silence greeted them in a stutter. The people were naked and brightly colored: some had painted tailcoats on themselves while others had painted uniforms which they themselves could never have seen. Humboldt's face lit up when he was told that this was a place where they prepared curare.

The curare master was a dignified, gaunt, priestly figure. This, he explained, was how the twigs were peeled, this was how the bark was rubbed on a stone, this was how — careful — the juice was poured into a funnel made from a banana leaf. The most important thing was the funnel. He doubted that Europe had produced anything so ingenious.

Well, yes, said Humboldt, it was certainly a perfectly respectable funnel.

And this, said the master, was how the stuff was evaporated in a clay vessel, please pay attention, even watching it was dangerous, and this was how the concentrated infusion of the leaves was added. And this, he held the little clay dish out to Humboldt, was now the strongest poison in this world and the other world too. It would kill angels!

Humboldt asked if one could drink it.

It was put on arrows, said the master. Nobody had ever tried to drink it. They weren't insane.

But people ate the animals killed by it right away?

Yes, said the master. That was the point.

Humboldt looked at his index finger. Then he stuck it in the bowl and licked it clean.

The master screamed.

Not to worry, said Humboldt. His finger was intact and so was the inside of his mouth. If one had no wounds, the stuff must not be deadly. The substance had to be researched, so he had to take the risk. But he must excuse himself, he was feeling a little weak. He sank to his knees and then remained sitting on the ground for some time, rubbing his forehead and humming to himself. Then he stood up with great care and bought all the master's supplies from him.

The onward journey was delayed for a day. Humboldt and Bonpland sat side by side on a fallen tree. Humboldt's eyes were fixed on his shoes, and Bonpland endlessly chanted the first line of a French counting rhyme. They knew now how curare was prepared, and together they had proved that one could ingest an astonishing amount by mouth without suffering worse effects than some dizziness and hallucinations, but that if even the tiniest amount was dripped into the blood, unconsciousness resulted and even a fifth of a gram was sufficient to kill a monkey, though the monkey could be saved by blowing air hard into its mouth for as long as the poison paralyzed its muscles. After an hour the effect would wear off, its capacity to move would gradually be restored, and there would be no ongoing effect except the ape would feel a bit sad. So they thought it must be a delusion when the bushes suddenly parted and a man with a mustache, wearing a linen shirt and a leather jacket, stepped out in front of them, sweaty but composed. He seemed to be in his mid-thirties, his name was Brombacher, and he was from Saxony. He didn't have plans and he wasn't going anywhere, he said, he just wanted to see the world.

Humboldt said why didn't he come with them.

Brombacher said thank you but no. One had more experiences on one's own and besides, home was full of nothing but Germans.

Stumblingly, out of practice in his mother tongue, Humboldt asked which town he was from, how high the church spire was, and how many people lived there.

Brombacher replied calmly and politely: Bad Kürthing, fifty-four feet, eight hundred and thirty-two souls. He offered them dirty flat cakes of dough; they declined. He told them about the wild game, the animals, and the lonely nights in the forest. After a short time he stood up, raised his hat to them, trudged off, and the foliage closed behind him. Among all the absurdities in his life, Humboldt wrote next day to his brother, this meeting was the most extraordinary. He would never be quite sure whether it had really happened or whether it had been a last after-effect of the poison on their imaginations.

Toward evening, the curare had passed off sufficiently for them to be able to move around, and they even felt hungry. The inhabitants of the mission were turning spits over a fire with the head of a child, three tiny hands, and four little feet with what were clearly toes. Not human, explained the missionary.

They stopped that wherever they could. Just little monkeys from the forest.

Bonpland refused to taste any. Humboldt hesitated, but took a hand and bit into it. It didn't taste bad but he didn't feel well. Would people be offended if he didn't eat it all?

The missionary shook his head, mouth full. Nobody would notice!

In the night, animal noises kept them awake. The imprisoned monkeys hammered against the bars and kept on screaming. Humboldt wrote the beginning of a treatise on night sounds of the forest and animal existence, which was to be understood as the continuation of an ongoing struggle, and consequently, the opposite of paradise.

He thought, said Bonpland, that the missionary had lied.

Humboldt looked up.

The man had been living here a long time, said Bonpland. The forest exerted enormous power. It must have been awkward for him, which is why he'd made his assertion. People here ate human flesh, was what Pater Zea had said, and everyone knew it. What could one missionary do against that?

Nonsense, said Humboldt.

No, said Julio, that sounded right.

Humboldt was silent for a moment. He begged their pardon, but they were all completely exhausted. He quite understood. But if any one of them said again that the godson of the Duke of Brunswick had eaten human flesh, he would reach for his weapon.

Bonpland laughed.

He meant it, said Humboldt.

No he didn't, said Bonpland.

Yes he did.

Everyone seemed uneasy and fell silent. Bonpland drew breath, but said nothing. One after the other they turned toward the fire and pretended to be asleep.

From now on Bonpland's fever began to get worse. More and more often he got up during the night, took a few steps, then collapsed, giggling to himself. Once Humboldt got the feeling that someone was bending over him. As if in a dream he saw Bonpland's face, teeth bared, a machete in his hand. He thought as fast as he could. One had strange dreams here, as he knew only too well. He needed Bonpland. So he had to trust him. This must therefore be a dream. He closed his eyes and forced himself to lie there motionless, until he heard the sound of footsteps. When he blinked the next time, Bonpland was lying beside him, eyes closed.

Day after day the hours blended into one another; the sun hung low and fiery over the river, it hurt to look at it, the mosquitoes attacked from every side, even the oarsmen were too exhausted to talk. For a time they were followed by a metal disc that flew ahead of them and then behind them again, glided silently through the sky, disappeared, reappeared, came so close for minutes at a time that Humboldt with his telescope could see the curved reflection of the river, their boat, and even himself in its glistening surface. Then it raced away and never came back.

The weather was clear when they reached the end of the channel. To the north, granite-white mountains reared over their heads, and on the other side grassy plains stretched away into the distance. Humboldt fixed the setting sun with his sextant and measured the angle between the path of Jupiter and that of the moon as it wandered on its way.

Now finally, he said, the channel really existed.

On the way back downstream, said Mario, things would go faster. No need to fear the rapids any more and they could stick to the middle of the river. And that way they'd escape the mosquitoes.

He doubted it, said Bonpland. He didn't believe there was a place anywhere that was free of them. They had even worked their way into his memory. If he thought of La Rochelle, he found the town full of insects.

The appearance of the channel on maps, said Humboldt, would benefit this entire part of the world. It would be possible to transport goods across the continent, new centers of trade would spring up, enterprises no one could ever dream of before would become possible.

Bonpland had a fit of coughing. Tears came pouring down his face and he spat up blood. There was nothing here, he panted. It was hotter than hell, there were nothing but stinks, mosquitoes, and snakes. There would never be anything here, and this filthy channel wouldn't make a bit of difference. Now could they please start back?

Humboldt stared at him for several moments. He hadn't decided that yet. The Esmeralda mission was the last Christian settlement before the wilderness. From there it would be a few weeks' journey through uncharted land to the Amazon. And nobody had yet discovered the Amazon's source.

Mario crossed himself.

On the other hand, said Humboldt reflectively, perhaps it would be imprudent. The thing might be dangerous. If he died now, all the findings and scientific results would die with him. No one would ever know about them.

They shouldn't be put at risk, said Bonpland.

It would be insanity, said Julio.

Not to mention those! Mario pointed to the corpses. No one would ever get to see them!

Humboldt nodded. Sometimes one had to be able to hold back.

The Esmeralda mission consisted of six houses set between huge stands of bananas. There wasn't even so much as a missionary, just an old Spanish soldier to oversee fifteen families of Indians. Humboldt engaged some of the men to scratch the termites out of the planks of the boat.

The decision not to go further was the right one, said the soldier. In the wilderness behind the mission the people were uninhibited murderers. They had several heads, they were immortal, and the language they spoke was Cat.

Humboldt sighed. He was troubled. It angered him that now some other person would find the source of the Amazon. To distract himself, he studied the paintings of suns, moons, and intricately coiled snakes that were scratched into the cliff almost three hundred feet above the river.

The water level must have been higher long ago, said the soldier.

Not that high, said Humboldt. Evidently the cliffs were once lower. He had a teacher in Germany whom he was hardly going to dare tell about this.

Or there were flying people, said the soldier.

Humboldt smiled.

Lots of creatures flew, said the soldier, and nobody thought that was odd. While on the other hand nobody had ever seen a mountain rising.

People didn't fly, said Humboldt. Even if he saw it, he wouldn't believe it.

And that was science?

Yes, said Humboldt, that was exactly what science was.

When the boat was repaired and Bonpland's fever had subsided, they started the return journey. As they said goodbye, the soldier asked Humboldt to put in a good word for him in the capital, so that he would be transferred elsewhere. It was unendurable. Just recently he'd found a spider in his food, and here he held both palms next to each other, that big! Twelve years, you couldn't expect that of anybody. Full of hope, he gave Humboldt two parrots as a gift and kept waving for a long time as they left.

Mario was right: going downstream was faster and out in midstream the insects weren't so aggressive. A short time later they reached the Jesuit mission, where Pater Zea greeted them with amazement.

He hadn't expected to see them again so soon. Remarkable robustness! And how had they got on with the cannibals?

He hadn't encountered any, said Humboldt.

Odd, said Pater Zea. Almost all the tribes up there were cannibals.

He couldn't confirm that, said Humboldt with a frown.

His people in the mission had been absolutely restless since their departure, said Pater Zea. They had been very stirred up by their ancestors being taken from their graves. Perhaps it would be better if they switched back into their old boat at once and continued their journey.

It looked as if a storm was coming, objected Humboldt.

This couldn't wait, said Pater Zea. Things were serious and he couldn't guarantee anything.

Humboldt thought for a moment. Then he said that they must obey authority.

The next afternoon clouds gathered. Thunder rumbled distantly over the plain, and suddenly they were plunged into the most cataclysmic storm they had ever encountered. Humboldt ordered the sail to be hauled down, and the chests, corpses, and animal cages unloaded onto a rocky island.

They'd had it coming, said Julio.

Rain had never yet hurt anybody, said Mario.

Rain hurt everyone, said Carlos. It could kill a person. It had already killed a lot of them.

They would never get home, said Julio.

And what if they did, said Mario. He'd never liked home.

Home, said Carlos, was death.

Humboldt instructed them to moor the boat over there against the other bank. They cast off and at that moment there was a surge in the river which carried the boat with it. For a moment, Bonpland and Humboldt saw one of the oars fly overboard, then the foaming water blocked their sight. Seconds later the boat flashed again a long way in the distance, then it and all four oarsmen were gone.

And now, asked Humboldt.

Since they were already here, said Bonpland, they could inspect the rocks.

A cavern led under one of the cataracts. Water thundered over their heads, and poured down in thick spouts through holes in the roof, but between them it was possible to stand dry. Hoarsely Bonpland suggested they measure the temperature.

Humboldt seemed to be exhausted. He couldn't explain, but sometimes he felt close to just letting go. Slowly he occupied himself with the instruments. And now, they must get out again — the cavern could flood at any moment!

They raced back into the open.

The rain was coming down even harder. The water poured down over them by the bucketful, soaked their clothes, filled their shoes, and made the ground so

133

slippery that it was hard to keep their footing. They sat down to wait. Crocodiles slid through the boiling water. The monkeys were roaring in their cages, pounding on the doors and pulling at the bars. The two parrots hung from their perches like dripping wet towels. One of them was staring miserably in front of it, while the other kept muttering curses in bad Spanish.

And what, asked Humboldt, if the boat didn't come back?

It would, said Bonpland, hush.

The rain came down even harder, as if the sky were trying to wash them off the island. The horizon flickered with lightning, and thunder broke over the cliffs on the other bank of the river, making the echo of each clap merge into the next.

This wasn't good, said Humboldt. They were surrounded by water, and they were sitting on the highest point. They must hope Mr. Franklin was wrong in his theory of lightning strikes.

Bonpland didn't say anything. He pulled out his flask and drank from it.

And he was surprised, said Humboldt, that there were so many lizards in among the rapids. It contradicted the suppositions of biology.

Bonpland took another swallow.

On the other hand there were known examples of fish that could even climb waterfalls.

Bonpland raised his eyebrows. The thunder had become a single, deafening, relentless uproar. At the other end of the island, not fifty feet away, something large and dark heaved itself onto the rock.

If they died, said Humboldt, nobody would know what had happened to them.

And if they did, said Bonpland, throwing away the empty flask, dead was dead.

Humboldt looked apprehensively at the crocodile. If they managed to return to the coast, he would send everything off to his brother: plants, maps, diaries, and collections. On two separate ships. Only then would he leave for the Cordilleras.

The Cordilleras?

Humboldt nodded. He would like to see the great volcanoes. The question of Neptunism had to get settled once and for all.

Soon they lost all sense of how long they had been waiting. Once a dead cow was propelled past them, then the lid of a piano, then a chessboard and a broken rocking chair. Humboldt carefully took out the clock, listened to its Parisian tick-tock, and peered at the hands through its waxed cloth cover. Either the storm had only begun a few minutes ago, or they'd been sitting fast for more than twelve hours, or then again perhaps the storm hadn't just wreaked chaos on river, forest, and sky, but on time itself; and simply washed away the hours, so that noon had now merged with the night and the following morning. Humboldt wrapped his arms around his knees.

Sometimes, he said, things made him wonder. By rights he should have been an inspector of mines. He would have lived in a German castle, had children, hunted deer on Sundays, and visited Weimar once a month. And now he was sitting here in the middle of a

135

flood, under foreign stars, waiting for a boat that would not come.

Bonpland asked if he thought he'd made a mistake. Castle, children, Weimar — that would be something!

Humboldt took off his hat, which the rain had reduced to a useless lump. A bat rose from the forest, was caught by the storm, forced down by the rain, and after a few wing beats was dragged away by the current.

The thought had never occurred to him.

Not even for a second?

Humboldt leaned forward to look at the crocodile. Then he shook his head.

The Stars

After he had announced where and when the planet would appear next time and of course nobody had believed him, and the poor lump of rock had materialized out of the night punctual to the very day and the very hour, he became famous. Astronomy was a popular branch of science. Kings involved themselves in it, generals followed its development, princes endowed prizes for discoveries, and the newspapers reported on Maskelyne, Mason, Dixon, and Piazzi as if they were heroes. A man who enlarged the horizons of mathematics forever was a curiosity. But a man who discovered a star was a made man.

Yes, said the duke, now it was obvious. Now he'd done it.

Gauss, who didn't know how to respond to this, said nothing and bowed.

And what else, asked the duke after the usual pause for reflection. Personally? He had heard there was a desire to marry?

Yes indeed, said Gauss, yes.

The audience chamber had changed. The mirror on the ceiling, obviously no longer in fashion, had been replaced by gold leaf, and there were fewer burning candles. Even the duke looked different: he had aged. One eyelid sagged, his cheeks were puffy, and his heavy body seemed to press painfully hard on his knees.

A tanner's daughter, if he was correct?

That was correct, said Gauss, and smiled as he added Your Highness. What a form of address! What a place. He must get hold of himself lest he become disrespectful. Yet he liked this duke. He wasn't a bad man, he tried to do things right and by comparison with most people he wasn't even stupid.

A family, said the duke, must be fed.

It couldn't be denied, said Gauss. Which is why he had dedicated himself to Ceres.

The duke looked at him, puzzled.

Gauss sighed. Ceres, he said slowly and clearly, was the name given to the planetoid that Piazzi had been the first to sight and whose orbit he, Gauss, had worked out. He had only applied himself to the problem because of his wedding plans. He had known that he needed to achieve something practical now that people could understand, even people who were less . . . He stopped. Even people who weren't interested in mathematics.

The duke nodded. Gauss remembered that he must not look at him directly, and dropped his gaze. He asked himself when the offer would finally be made. Always this boring to-ing and fro-ing, always these circumlocutions. All this time wasted in chatter!

Along these lines, he had an idea, said the duke.

Gauss's eyebrows shot up, miming surprise. He knew the idea was Zimmerman's, who had spent hours talking to the duke.

Perhaps it had occurred to him that Brunswick still had no observatory.

None too soon, said Gauss.

Pardon?

It had occurred to him.

Now he was wondering if the town shouldn't have one. And Doctor Gauss, despite his youth, should become its first director. The duke put his hands on his hips, and his face broadened into a big smile. That would surprise him now, wouldn't it?

He wanted the title of professor to go with it, said Gauss.

The duke said nothing.

The title of professor, said Gauss again, enunciating every syllable. An appointment at the University of Helmstadt. A salary twice a month.

The duke paced up and down, made a noise between a rumble and a hum, looked at the gold-leaf ceiling. Gauss used the time to count off some prime numbers. He already had thousands of them. In fact he was sure that there would never be a formula to determine them. But if one counted off several hundred thousand, one could establish the likelihood of their occurrence asymptomatically. For a moment he was concentrating so hard that he jumped when the duke said that one didn't bargain with one's ruling prince.

He had no such intention, said Gauss. On the other hand he felt it incumbent on him to admit that he had received an offer from Berlin and another from the Academy of St. Petersburg. Russia had always interested him. He had often thought about learning the Russian language.

Petersburg, said the duke, was a long way away. Berlin wasn't nearby either. If one thought about it, the nearest place was right here. Every other place was somewhere else. Even Göttingen. He was no scientist so he begged to be corrected if he was mistaken.

Indeed, said Gauss, eyes fixed on the floor. That was correct.

And if one wasn't held back by love of one's native land, one could at least reflect on the fact that travel was exhausting. One must make a home elsewhere, one had worries, moving cost money and was a hideous operation. And perhaps one also had an aged mother at home.

Gauss felt himself go red. It always happened when someone mentioned his mother; not out of shame, but because he loved her so much. Nevertheless, he had to clear his throat and say it again: nevertheless, one couldn't always do what one wanted. If one had a family, one needed money, and one had to go wherever it was to be found.

One would find some agreement, said the duke. The title of professor would be possible. Even if not with a twice-monthly salary.

But what if one wanted the title because of the salary?

Then one would not be doing honor to one's profession, said the duke coolly.

Gauss realized he had gone too far. He bowed, the duke dismissed him with a gesture, and a servant immediately opened a door behind him.

While waiting for the written offer from the Court, he busied himself with the art of calculating orbits. The path of a star, he said to Johanna, was not just merely a movement, it was the necessary result of the influence that all bodies exerted on a single body in the void: the line, in other words, that was formed with exactly the same curve on paper and in space, when one hurled an object into the void. The riddle of gravity. The tenacious attraction of all bodies.

The attraction of bodies, she repeated and struck him on the shoulder with her fan. He tried to kiss her, she retreated laughing. He had never found out why she had changed her mind. Since her second letter, she had behaved as if it were the most self-explanatory thing on earth. And he liked it that there were things he didn't understand.

Two days before the wedding he rode to Göttingen, to visit Nina one last time.

You're getting married now, she said, and not to me, naturally.

No, he replied, naturally not.

She asked if he hadn't loved her.

A little, he said, as he loosened the ties on her dress and simply couldn't believe that in two days' time he'd be doing this with Johanna. But he was going to keep his other promise, he was going to learn Russian. And although she swore it meant nothing, in her profession you became sentimental, it amazed and also displeased him that she was weeping.

The horse snorted angrily when he pulled it to a halt out in the open country on the way home. He had realized how to derive Jupiter's mass from the distortions in Ceres' orbit. He looked up into the night sky until his neck hurt. Even recently there had been nothing there but glowing points of light. Now he could distinguish their formations, he knew which of them marked the most important degrees of latitude for ocean navigation, he knew their paths, the times of their disappearance and reappearance. Spontaneously and apparently merely because he needed money, they had become his calling and he had become their reader.

There were not many guests at the wedding: his old father, now very bent, his mother, weeping like a child, Martin Bartels, and Professor Zimmerman, plus Johanna's family, her horrible friend Minna, and a secretary from the Court who seemed to have no idea why he had been sent. During the frugal celebratory dinner, Gauss's father made a speech saying that one should never be forced to bow, not to anyone, ever, then Zimmerman got up, opened his mouth, smiled adorably at everyone, and sat down again. Bartels nudged Gauss.

He stood up, swallowed, and said he had not expected to find anything like happiness, and fundamentally, he didn't believe in it even now. It seemed to him to be something like a mistake in arithmetic, an error, and he could only hope he would not be caught out. He sat down again and was surprised to see people looking blank. Quietly he asked Johanna if he had said something wrong.

In what way, she replied. It was exactly the speech she had always dreamed of for her wedding.

An hour later the last guests had left and he and Johanna were on their way home. They said little. Suddenly they were strangers to each other.

In the bedroom he closed the curtains, went to her, felt her instinctively want to pull back, held her gently but firmly, and began to undo her dress. Without any light, it wasn't easy. Nina had always worn clothes that made things simpler. It took a long time, the material was so resistant and there were so many fastenings that he himself could hardly believe that he still hadn't got it all undone. But then it finally worked, the dress fell to the floor and her naked shoulders gleamed white in the darkness. He put his arm around her shoulders, she instinctively covered her breasts with her hands, and he felt her holding back as he led her to the bed. He wondered how he should proceed with her petticoat, the dress had already been difficult enough. Why didn't women wear things one could open? Don't be frightened, he whispered and was surprised when she answered that she wasn't, and reached for his belt with a sure hand and a purposefulness that nothing had prepared him for. Have you done this before? What did he think of her, she asked, laughing, and next moment her petticoat was billowing on the floor, and she hesitated, so he pulled her with him so that they were lying together, breathing heavily, and each of them was waiting for the other's heartbeat to slow down. As he let

143

his hand slide over her breasts to her stomach and then, he decided to dare it even though he felt he should apologize, on further down, a sliver of moon appeared between the curtains, pale and watery, and he was ashamed to realize that in this very moment he suddenly understood how to make approximate corrections in mismeasurements of the trajectories of planets. He wished he could jot it down, but now her hand was creeping down his back. She had not imagined it was like this, she said with a mixture of fear and fascination, so full of life, as if there were a third creature with them. He threw himself on her, felt her shock, paused for a moment, then she wound her legs around his body, but he apologized, got up, stumbled to the desk, dipped the pen, and without lighting a candle wrote *sum of square of diff. betw. obs'd and calc'd>Min*. It was too important, he couldn't forget it. He heard her say she couldn't believe it, and she wasn't believing it either even though it was happening right in front of her. But he was already done. On the way back he hit his foot against the bedpost, then he felt her underneath him again, and it was only when she pulled him close that he realized how nervous he actually was, and for a moment it seemed astonishing that the two of them, who hardly knew each other, were now in this situation. Then something else happened and he was not shy any more, and toward dawn they were so well acquainted that they might have been practicing with each other forever.

Did happiness make one stupid? When he leafed through the *Disquisitiones* in the following weeks, he couldn't quite believe that the book was by him. He had to pull himself together before he could understand all the derivatives. He wondered if his intellect was sinking into mediocrity. Astronomy was a cruder science than mathematics. One couldn't solve the problems by pure thought; someone had to stare through an eyepiece until his eyes hurt while someone else had to tabulate the resulting measurements at mind-numbing length. The person who did this for him was a Herr Bessel in Bremen, whose only talent lay in the fact that he never ever made mistakes. As director of an observatory, Gauss had the right to requisition assistance — even if the foundation stone of this observatory hadn't even been laid yet.

He had asked for an audience more than once, but the duke was always busy. He wrote a furious letter and received no reply. He wrote a second, and when there was still no response to this, he waited so long outside the audience chamber that a secretary with tousled hair and untidy uniform eventually had to send him home. On the street he met Zimmerman and complained bitterly.

The professor looked at him as if he were an apparition and asked if he were really oblivious that there was a war on.

Gauss looked around. The street lay quiet in the sunshine, a baker was passing by with a basket of bread, the tin weathercock glinted dully above the church roof. The air smelled of lilacs. War?

It was true that he hadn't read a newspaper for weeks. Bartels hoarded everything. He went to his house and seated himself in front of a stack of old journals. Grimly he leafed past a report of Alexander von Humboldt's about the highlands of Caxamarca. Was there any damn place this fellow hadn't been? But just as he reached the war reports, he was interrupted by the crunching wheels of a column of wagons. Bayonets, cavalry helmets, and lances paraded past the window for the next half hour. Bartels came home panting to announce that the duke was lying in one of the coaches, shot at Jena, bleeding like an ox, and dying. Everything was lost.

Gauss folded the newspaper. In that case he could go home.

He mustn't say it to anyone, but this Bonaparte interested him. Supposedly he dictated up to six letters at the same time. Once he had found an outstanding solution to the problem of how to divide a circle with fixed compasses. He won battles by being the first to announce with absolute authority that he'd won them. He thought faster and deeper than other people, that was his whole secret. Gauss wondered if Napoleon had ever heard of him.

The observatory was not going to come to anything, he told Johanna at supper. He would have to keep observing the sky from his parlor, a complete disgrace. He had an offer from Göttingen. They wanted to build an observatory there too, it wasn't far away, and from there he could visit his mother every week. They could do the move before the baby arrived.

But Göttingen, said Johanna, now belonged to France.

Belonged to France?

How could he, of all people, be so blind to things that were obvious to everyone else? Göttingen belonged to Hannover, whose personal union with the English crown had been broken by the French victory, and Napoleon had now attached it to the new kingdom of Westphalia, to be ruled by Jérôme Bonaparte. So to whom would a Westphalian official swear his oath of office? Napoleon!

He rubbed his forehead. Westphalia, he repeated, as if it would become clearer if he said it out loud, Jérôme. What did that have to do with them?

With Germany, she said, it had to do with Germany and with where one stood.

He looked at her helplessly.

She already knew, she exclaimed, what he was going to say — that looked at from the future, both sides would cancel each other out and before long nobody would be getting excited about the things people were dying for today. But what difference did that make? Cozying up to the future was a form of cowardice. Did he really think that people would be more intelligent then?

Yes, a little, he said. Of necessity.

But we're living right now!

Unfortunately, he said, snuffed the candles, went to the telescope, and focused it on the overcast surface of Jupiter. The night was clear, and he could see its tiny moons more distinctly than ever before.

Soon afterward he presented the telescope to Professor Pfaff and they moved to Göttingen. Here

147

there was general chaos. French soldiers racketed around at night and on the site of the future observatory, ground hadn't even been broken for the foundations, and the occasional sheep munched on the grass. He had to observe the stars from Professor Lichtenberg's old tower room above the town wall. And worst of all: he was forced to give seminars. Young men came to his apartments, rocked on his chairs, and left grease spots on the cushions of his sofa while he labored to make them understand anything at all.

His students were the stupidest people he had ever met. He spoke so slowly that he had forgotten the beginning of his sentences before he'd reached the end. It didn't do any good. He left everything difficult out, and stuck to the absolute basics. They didn't understand. He wanted to cry. He wondered if halfwits had a special idiom that one could learn like a foreign language. He gesticulated with both hands, pointed to his lips, and shaped sounds exaggeratedly, as if he were dealing with the deaf. But the only person to pass the examination was a young man with watery eyes. His name was Moebius, and he was the only one who appeared not to be a cretin. When he was the only one again to pass the second examination, the dean took Gauss aside after the faculty meeting and begged him not to be so strict. When Gauss got home close to tears, he found only uninvited strangers: a doctor, a midwife, and his parents-in-law.

He'd missed everything, said his mother-in-law. Head in the clouds again!

He didn't even have a decent telescope, he said, upset. What had happened?

It was a boy.

What did she mean, a boy? Only when he saw her eyes did he understand. And he knew at once that she would never forgive him.

He was distressed that he found it so hard to like the baby. People had said it happened of its own accord. But weeks after the birth, when he held the helpless creature who for some reason was called Joseph in his hands and looked at his tiny nose and disconcertingly complete tally of toes, all he felt was pity and shyness. Johanna took it away from him and asked with sudden concern whether he was happy. Of course, he said, and went to his telescope.

Since they had moved to Göttingen, he was visiting Nina again. She was no longer so young, and received him with the intimacy of a wife. He still hadn't learned Russian, she said reproachfully, and he apologized and promised to do it soon. He had sworn to himself that Johanna would never know of these visits, he would lie even under torture. It was his duty to keep pain from her. It was not his duty to tell her the truth. Knowledge was painful. There wasn't a day he didn't wish he had less of it.

He had begun a work of astronomy. Nothing important, not a book for the ages like the *Disquisitiones*, it would be overtaken in time. But it promised to be the most accurate guide to the calculation of orbits and trajectories there had ever been. And he had to hurry. Although he had just turned thirty, he noticed that his concentration was slipping and the pauses that people seemed to make before replying to something were getting shorter. He had lost some more of his teeth, and from week to week he was plagued by colic. The doctor advised smoking a pipe every morning and a lukewarm bath before going to bed. He was sure he would never achieve old age. When Johanna told him that another child was on the way, he couldn't have said whether he was pleased or not. It would have to grow up without him, that much was clear. He was anxious during the birth and relieved afterwards, and in honor of her stupid friend Minna the baby was named Wilhelmine. When he tried to teach her to count a few months later, Johanna said it was really too early.

Unwillingly, because Johanna was already pregnant again, he went to Bremen to go through the Jupiter tabulations with Bessel. During the week before the journey he slept badly, had nightmares, and was irritable and depressed for days. The journey was even worse than the one to Königsberg, the coach even narrower, his fellow travelers even more unwashed, and when a wheel broke, they had to stand for four hours in a muddy landscape while the cursing driver repaired it. The moment that Gauss, exhausted, with a heavy head and a sore back, had climbed out of the coach, Bessel asked him about the calculation of Jupiter's mass from the disturbances in Ceres' trajectory. Had he worked out a consistent orbit yet?

Gauss saw red. He didn't have it yet, what could he do! He had spent hundreds of hours on it. The thing was unimaginably difficult, a torture, dammit he wasn't young any more, people should spare him, in any case he didn't have long to live, it had been a mistake to launch himself on this rubbish in the first place.

Very subdued, Bessel asked if he'd like to see the sea.

No expeditions, said Gauss.

It was really close, said Bessel. A mere stroll! In fact it was another laborious journey and the coach rocked so violently that Gauss got his colic again. It was raining, the window didn't shut tight, and they were soaked to the skin.

But it was worth it, Bessel kept saying. The sea was something one had to see.

Had to? Gauss asked where that was written.

The beach was dirty and even the water left something to be desired. The horizon seemed narrow, the sky was low, and the sea looked like soup under a scum of mist. A cold wind blew. Something was burning nearby and the smoke made it hard to breathe. The body of a headless chicken washed up and down in the waves.

Fine. Gauss blinked into the haze. And now they could go home, yes?

But Bessel's entrepreneurial spirit was unbounded. It wasn't enough to see the sea, one also had to go to the theater!

The theater was expensive, said Gauss.

Bessel laughed. The professor should consider himself a guest, it would be his honor. He would hire a private coach, they would be there in no time at all!

The journey took four agonizing days and the bed at the inn in Weimar was so hard that Gauss's back pain became unbearable. Besides which the bushes along the Ilm made him sneeze. The court theater was hot, and sitting for hours a trial. The play being performed was a piece by Voltaire. Somebody killed somebody else. A woman cried. A man complained. Another woman fell to her knees. There were monologues. The translation was elegant and melodic, but Gauss would rather have read it. He yawned till the tears ran down his cheeks.

Moving, wasn't it, whispered Bessel.

The actors flung their hands up in the air, paced endlessly back and forth, and rolled their eyes as they spoke.

He thought, whispered Bessel, that Goethe was in his box today.

Gauss asked if that was the ass who considered himself fit to correct Newton's theory of light.

People turned around. Bessel seemed to shrink into his seat and didn't say another word until the curtain fell.

As they were leaving, a gaunt gentleman came to speak to them. Did he have the honor to be addressing Gauss the astronomer?

The astronomer and mathematician, said Gauss.

The man introduced himself as a Prussian diplomat, currently posted to Rome, but en route to Berlin where he would take up a position as director of education in the Interior Ministry. There was a great deal to do, the German educational system needed to be reformed from the ground up. He himself had enjoyed the finest education, now he had the opportunity to offer some of it to others. He stood very straight, without leaning on his silver stick. Moreover, they were alumni of the same university and had acquaintances in common. That Herr Gauss was also active in mathematics was something he hadn't known. Uplifting, wasn't it!

Gauss didn't understand.

The performance.

Oh, yes, said Gauss.

The gentleman understood perfectly. Not quite the right thing at this moment. Something German would have been more appropriate. But it was hard to argue with Goethe about such matters.

Gauss, who hadn't been listening up till now, asked the diplomat to repeat his name.

The diplomat bowed and did so. He too was a scientist!

Curious, Gauss leant forward.

He researched old languages.

Ah, said Gauss.

That, said the diplomat, sounded rather disappointed.

Linguistics. Gauss shook his head. He didn't wish to be offensive.

No, no. He should say it.

Gauss shrugged. Linguistics was for people who had the precision for mathematics but not the intelligence. People who would invent their own makeshift logic.

The diplomat was silent.

Gauss asked him about his travels. He must have been everywhere!

153

That, said the diplomat sourly, was the other von Humboldt, his brother. A case of mistaken identity, and not the first time it had happened. He said goodbye and left with small steps.

That night the pain in his back and stomach gave Gauss no rest. He twisted and turned this way and that and quietly cursed his fate, Weimar, and most of all Bessel. Early next morning, Bessel wasn't yet awake, he ordered the coach to be hitched up, and instructed the driver to take him to Göttingen at once.

When he finally arrived, his traveling case still in his hand, alternately bent double because of his stomach pains and leaning over backwards at an awkward angle to ease his spine, he went to the university to enquire when construction would begin on the observatory.

There wasn't much sound from the ministry right now, said the official. Hannover was a long way away. Nobody knew anything precise. In case he had forgotten, there was a war on.

The army had ships, said Gauss, ships needed to be sailed, navigation needed astronomical charts, and astronomical charts weren't so easy to make at home in the kitchen.

The official promised to have news soon. What was more, there were plans to resurvey the kingdom of Westphalia. The herr professor had already done work as a geodetic surveyor. They were looking for an industrious person who could count, to be leader of the enterprise.

Gauss opened his mouth. Using every ounce of willpower he managed not to scream at the man. He closed his mouth again and left without saying goodbye.

He wrenched open the door to his apartments, called out that he was home and wouldn't be leaving again any time soon. He was pulling off his boots in the hall when the doctor, the midwife, and his mother-in-law stepped out of the bedroom. Ah, wonderful, this time he wouldn't have to reproach himself. Smiling broadly, a little too exuberantly, he asked if it had arrived yet and if it was a boy or a girl and most of all, how much it weighed.

A boy, said the doctor. He was dying. As was his mother.

They had tried everything, said the midwife.

What happened after that was beyond his capacity to recall clearly. It seemed as if time were racing both forwards and backwards, and multiple possibilities had simultaneously opened and closed. One memory had him at Johanna's bedside, as she opened her eyes for a moment and gave him a look that was empty of all recognition. Her hair was sticking to her face, her hand was damp and limp, the basket with the infant was standing next to his chair. This was contradicted by another memory in which she was no longer conscious when he stormed into the room, and a third, in which she died at that very moment, her body pale and wax-like, and a fourth in which the two of them had an appallingly clear conversation: she asked if she had to die, after a moment's hesitation he nodded, whereupon she told him not to be sad for too long, one lived, then one died, that was how it was. Only after six o'clock in the afternoon did things come together again. He was sitting at her bedside. People were whispering in the hall. Johanna was dead.

He pushed back the chair and tried to accustom himself to the thought that he would have to marry again. He had children. He had no idea how one brought them up. He couldn't run a household. Servants cost money.

Quietly he opened the door. This, he thought, is it. Having to live although everything was over. Arranging things, organizing things: every day, every hour, every minute. As if there were still some sense in it.

He was a little comforted when he heard his mother arrive. He thought of the stars. The short formula that would summarize all their movements in a simple line. For the first time he knew it would always elude him. Darkness fell slowly. And slowly he moved toward the telescope.

The Mountain

By the light of a guttering oil lamp, while the wind blew past carrying more and more snowflakes, Aimé Bonpland was trying to write a letter home. If he thought about the preceding months, it was as if he'd lived dozens of lives, all of them similar to one another and none of them worth repeating. The journey up the Orinoco seemed like something one read about in books, New Andalusia was a prehistoric legend, Spain no more than a mere word. He had begun to feel better meanwhile, some days he was already free of fever, and even the dreams, in which he strangled, dismembered, shot, burned, poisoned, or buried Baron Humboldt under stones, were becoming less frequent.

He paused for thought, and chewed the end of his quill. Somewhat higher up the mountain, surrounded by sleeping mules, his hair covered with hoarfrost and a little snow, Humboldt was working out their position using the moons of Jupiter. He had the glass cylinder of the barometer balanced on his knees. Beside him, wrapped in blankets, their three mountain guides were asleep.

Next day, wrote Bonpland, they wanted to conquer Chimborazo. In case they didn't survive, Baron Humboldt had advised him most insistently to write a letter of farewell, because it was beneath a man to die just like that, without a final word to anyone. On the mountain they would collect rocks and plants, even up here there were unknown plants, he had harvested far too many of them these last months. The baron maintained there were only sixteen underlying species, but the baron was good at recognizing species whereas he, Bonpland, couldn't care less. The majority of their specimens, including three very ancient corpses, had been loaded in Havana onto a ship bound for France, and in a second ship they had sent the herb collections and all their written records to Baron Humboldt's brother. Three weeks ago, or maybe it was six, the days went by so quickly and he had lost all perspective, they had learned that one of the ships had sunk. That had cost Baron Humboldt some bad days, but then he'd said they were only just starting. He, Bonpland, had been less upset by the loss, as he was running such a fever at the time that he hardly knew where and why and who he was. Most of the time he had been fighting flies and mechanical spiders in his nightmares. He was trying not to think about it, and hoped the ship that sank hadn't been the one with the corpses. He had spent so much time with them that by the time they got back to the mouth of the river, he felt they weren't just ballast, but silent companions.

Bonpland wiped his brow and took a deep mouthful from his brass flask. Earlier on he had had a silver one, but he'd lost it under circumstances he could no longer remember. They were only just starting, he wrote. Then he noticed that he'd used this same sentence twice, and crossed it out. They were only just starting! He blinked and crossed it out again. Unfortunately he couldn't describe the details of their route, everything was a blur, all he had was a couple of images which seemed, if he really tried, to have some connection. In Havana, for example, the baron had had two crocodiles captured and shut in with a pack of dogs to study their hunting behavior. The screaming of the dogs had been almost unbearable, it sounded like children crying. And afterwards the walls had been so bloody that the room had had to be repainted at Baron Humboldt's expense.

He closed his eyes, then snapped them open again and looked all round him in surprise, as if he had forgotten for a moment where he was. He coughed and took another large mouthful. Off Cartagena their ship had almost capsized, and on the river Magdalena the mosquitoes had plagued them even more determinedly than on the Orinoco; finally they had climbed thousands of steps once laid by the long-lost Incas to the freezing heights of the Cordilleras. Normally people would have been carried up by porters but Baron Humboldt had refused. Because of human dignity. The porters had been so insulted they had almost beaten them to a pulp. Bonpland took a deep breath; then, involuntarily, he sighed quietly. Outside Santa Fé de Bogotá the town dignitaries had been gathered to greet them, their fame had already gone before them, at least that of the baron, whereas strangely enough, nobody seemed to have heard of Aimé Bonpland. Maybe this had to do with the fever. He stopped: the last sentence struck him as illogical. He considered whether to cross it out, but then decided against it. Their hosts had been noble people, there was laughter when the baron had refused to let go of his barometer, and they seemed amazed that so famous a man could be so short. They had been given hospitality by Mutis, the biologist. The baron had always kept trying to talk about plants, but Mutis's invariable response was that one did not discuss such subjects in society. Nonetheless, he, Bonpland, had succeeded in reducing his fever thanks to Mutis's herbs. Mutis had employed a young chambermaid, an Indian from the highlands, with whom, here he paused, took a large gulp, and peered up at Humboldt's figure, now almost invisible in the darkness, he could have excellent social intercourse of this, that, and indeed every other kind. Meanwhile the baron had inspected mines and drawn maps. Outstanding maps. Of that he had no doubt.

He nodded several times unconsciously, then continued. They had advanced with eleven mules across the river and up the route to the pass. Pouring rain. The ground boggy and full of thorns. And because Baron Humboldt also refused to allow himself to be carried, they had had to go barefoot to spare their boots. They had walked their feet to a bloody mess. And the mules had been obstreperous. They had had to stop climbing Pichincha when he was overcome with dizziness and nausea. At first Baron Humboldt had wanted to carry on alone, but then he too had passed out. Somehow they had made it back down into the valley. The baron had then tried it again with a guide who of course had never been up there in his life, in these parts nobody went climbing mountains unless someone forced them to. It took three tries before they were successful, and now they knew exactly how high the mountain was, the temperature of its smoke, and the identity of the lichens on its stones. Baron Humboldt was exceedingly interested in volcanoes, more than anything else, it all had to do with his teachers in Germany and a man in Weimar he revered like a god. Now they were facing their crowning enterprise. Chimborazo. Bonpland took a last swallow, wrapped himself tighter in his coverlet, and looked out at Humboldt, who, as he could just still make out, was listening to the ground with a brass cone.

He had heard a rumbling, Humboldt called. Movements in the earth's crust! With any luck they could hope for an eruption.

That would be wonderful, said Bonpland, folded the letter, and stretched out on the floor. He felt the chill of the frozen earth against his cheek. It seemed to ease his fever.

As always, he went to sleep at once, and as he almost always did, he dreamed that he was in Paris, it was morning sometime in the fall, and rain was pattering gently against the windowpane. A woman he couldn't see clearly asked if he really did believe he'd traveled through the tropics and he answered not really, and if he had, then it was only for a moment. Then he woke up because Humboldt was shaking his shoulder and

161

asking what he was waiting for, it was already past four o'clock. Bonpland stood up and as Humboldt turned away, he seized him, pushed him toward the ravine, and threw him with all his strength over the edge of the cliff. Someone shook his shoulder and asked what he was waiting for, it was four o'clock, they had to leave. Bonpland rubbed his eyes, brushed the snow out of his hair, and stood up.

The Indian guides looked at him sleepily, and Humboldt handed them a sealed envelope. His farewell letter to his brother. He had spent a long time polishing it. In case he should not return, he asked their assurance that they would bring it to the nearest Jesuit mission.

The guides yawned and said yes.

And this was his, said Bonpland. It wasn't sealed, they could read it if they wished, and if they didn't deliver it, he really didn't care.

Humboldt ordered the guides to wait for them for at least three days. They nodded, bored, and twitched their woolen ponchos straight. Meticulously he checked over the chronometer and the telescope, then crossed his arms and stared into space for a time. Suddenly, he left. Hastily Bonpland seized specimen boxes and stick and ran after him.

More at ease than he'd been for a long time, Humboldt talked about his childhood, working on the lightning conductor, the lonely excursions through the woods, and afterwards arranging his first beetles in collections, and Henriette Herz's salon. He pitied

162

anyone who had not been graced with such a sentimental education.

His sentimental education, said Bonpland, had taken place with a farm girl from the neighborhood. She had allowed just about everything. He'd had to protect himself from her brothers, that was all.

He kept thinking about the dog, said Humboldt suddenly. He still couldn't get rid of his sense of guilt. He had been responsible for the beast!

The farm girl had been astonishing. Not even fourteen, and she had mastered things you wouldn't believe.

The dogs in Havana had been another matter. Of course he had been sorry about them. But science demanded it, and now one knew more about the hunting habits of crocodiles. Besides which, they'd been mongrels, no pedigrees, and very mangy.

Where they were going now, there were no more plants, only brownish yellow lichens on the stones poking up out of the snow. Bonpland heard his own heart beating very loud and the hissing of the wind as it swept over the surfaces of the snow. When a little butterfly flew up in front of him, he felt a shock.

Panting, Humboldt came to the topic of Urquijo's fall from grace. A bad business. It was still a rumor, but gradually the signs were accumulating that the minister had lost the favor of the queen. Which meant more decades of slavery. When they got back, he intended to write some things that these people were not going to like.

163

The snow piled higher. Bonpland lost his footing and slid downhill, followed shortly afterwards by Humboldt. To protect the scrapes on their hands from the cold, they wrapped them in scarves. Humboldt examined the leather soles of his shoes. Nails, he said thoughtfully. Driven through the soles from the inside out. That's what they needed now.

Soon the snow was up to their knees and a sudden mist enveloped them. Humboldt measured the dips in the magnetic needle and established their altitude with the barometer. If he wasn't mistaken, the shortest route to the summit led northeast over the flattened slope, then a bit to the left, then steep uphill.

Northeast, Bonpland repeated. In this mist you couldn't even tell where the summit and the valley were!

There, said Humboldt, and pointed off somewhere with absolute assurance.

Bent over, they trudged past walls of cliff that had cracked and weathered into columns. High above them, visible for seconds then hidden again, a snow-covered ridge led up to the top. Instinctively, they bore to the left as they walked, where the land fell away steeply in sheets of frost. To their right, it was a straight drop into the abyss. At first Bonpland was oblivious to the gentleman in dark clothes trudging sadly at their side. Only when the figure transformed itself into a geometrical shape, a kind of pulsating honeycomb, did he feel uneasy.

Left, over there, he asked, was that something?

Humboldt glanced to the side. No.

Good, said Bonpland.

They paused for a rest on a narrow platform because Bonpland's nose was bleeding. Uneasily he looked around at the honeycomb, which was swaying slowly toward them. He coughed and took a mouthful from his brass flask. When the bleeding let up and they were able to continue, he felt relieved. Humboldt's timepiece told them that they had only been climbing for a few hours. The mist was so thick that there was no way to tell up from down: wherever one looked, there was a single unbroken expanse of white.

The snow was now up to their hips. Humboldt cried out and vanished into a drift. Bonpland dug with his hands until he got hold of his coat, and pulled him out. Humboldt thumped the snow off his clothes and satisfied himself that none of the instruments were damaged. They found an outcrop of rock where they waited for the mists to thin and brighten. Soon the sun would break through.

Old friend, said Humboldt. He didn't want to turn sentimental, but after the long way they'd come, at a great moment like this, there was something he wanted to say.

Bonpland listened. But nothing came out. Humboldt seemed to have forgotten already.

He didn't wish to be a spoilsport, said Bonpland, but something was wrong. There, to the right, no, a bit further on, no, left, yes, that was it. That thing that looked like a star made of cotton wool. Or like a house.

165

Was he right to assume that he was the only one who could see it?

Humboldt nodded.

Bonpland asked if he should be worried.

Matter of opinion, said Humboldt. It was probably the result of reduced pressure and the altered composition of the air. Noxious gases could be excluded. But besides, he wasn't the doctor here.

So who else was?

Intriguing, said Humboldt, how constantly the density of the atmosphere lessened as one went up. If one did the math, one could deduce at what point the void began. Or at what point, because of the drop in boiling point, the blood began to bubble in the veins. As for himself, for example, he'd been seeing the lost dog for quite some time. He looked completely ragged, and he was missing a leg and an ear. Aside from that, he didn't sink into the snow at all, and his eyes were black and dead. It wasn't a pretty sight, and he was having to keep a tight hold on himself to keep from screaming. Nor could he stop thinking about the fact that they'd failed to give the dog a name. But maybe that hadn't been necessary, they'd only had the one dog, right?

He didn't know of any other, said Bonpland.

Humboldt, comforted, gave a nod and they kept climbing. They had to move slowly because of the crevasses under the snow. Once the mist lightened for a few seconds and there was a ravine right there, then the mist covered it again. Bleeding from the gums,

166

Humboldt said to himself reproachfully, no fit condition, should be ashamed of himself.

Bonpland's nose was also bleeding again, and despite the wrappings he had no feeling in his hands any more. He excused himself, then sank to his knees and vomited.

Cautiously they clambered up a steep wall of rock. Bonpland thought of the day on the island in the Orinoco when they had been trapped by the rain. How had they actually got away? He couldn't remember. Just as he was about to ask Humboldt, the latter's foot dislodged a stone which hit him on the shoulder. It hurt so much that he almost lost his hand-holds. He closed his eyes tight and rubbed snow into his face. After that he felt better, except that the pulsing honeycomb still hung beside him and, even more unpleasant, every time he tried to grip on to the rock face, it pulled away from him a little. Now and again, weathered faces peered at him out of the cliff, looking half-decomposed, or bored. Luckily the mist made it impossible to see down.

That time on the island, in the river, he called. How did they actually get away?

The answer was so long in coming that Bonpland had completely forgotten the question when Humboldt eventually turned his head toward him. He couldn't remember for the life of him. So how did they?

At the top of the rock face the mist parted. They saw some snatches of blue sky and the cone of the summit. The cold air was very thin: no matter how deeply they breathed, almost nothing entered their lungs. Bonpland tried to take his pulse, but kept miscounting until eventually he gave up. They found a narrow bridge of rock covered with snow that led over a crevasse.

Look ahead, said Humboldt, never look down!

Bonpland immediately looked down. He felt the whole perspective shift as the floor of the ravine came hurtling up toward him and the bridge plunged downwards. Terrified, he clung to his stick. The bridge, he stuttered.

Keep moving, said Humboldt.

No rock, said Bonpland.

Humboldt stopped. It was true: there was no stone beneath them. They were on a freestanding bridge of snow. He stared down.

Don't think, said Bonpland. Keep moving.

Keep moving, repeated Humboldt, not moving an inch.

Just go, said Bonpland.

Humboldt set off again.

Bonpland set one foot in front of the other. For what seemed hours he heard the snow crunching and knew that the only thing between him and the abyss was water crystals. Right until the very end of his life, destitute and a prisoner in the loneliness of Paraguay, he would be able to recall these images in the smallest detail: the little clouds of mist dispersing, the bright air, the ravine at the bottom of his field of vision. He tried to hum a song, but the voice he heard wasn't his, and so he let it go. Ravine, summit, sky, and crunching snow, and they still hadn't reached the other side. And still not. Until at some point, Humboldt was already waiting and reached out a hand toward him. And he made it.

Bonpland, said Humboldt. He looked small and gray and suddenly old.

Humboldt, said Bonpland.

For a while they stood side by side, saying nothing. Bonpland pressed a handkerchief against his bleeding nose. Gradually, transparent at first but then more and more clearly, the pulsating honeycomb retreated. The snow bridge was ten feet long, fifteen at the most, and crossing it could only have taken a matter of seconds.

Testing every step, they moved along the ridge. Bonpland worked out that he was apparently three people: one who was walking, one who was watching the first one walking, and one who kept up a running commentary in a totally incomprehensible language. By way of an experiment, he slapped his own face. That helped a little and for a few minutes he was thinking more clearly. It just didn't change the fact that where the sky ought to be, there was ground, and that they were climbing downhill upside down.

But it did make sense, said Bonpland loudly. After all, they were on the other side of the earth.

He couldn't understand Humboldt's answer, because it was drowned out by the babbling commentary of the man accompanying him. Bonpland began to sing. First one, then the other of the men accompanying them joined in. Bonpland had learned the song at school, and was pretty sure that no one else in this hemisphere would know it. A proof that the two men at his side were real and not swindlers, because who could have taught it to them? Admittedly something in this thought wasn't quite logical, but he couldn't work out what. And finally it didn't matter, as there was no guarantee that he was the person having these thoughts, and not one of the other two. His breath came short and loud, and his heart was pounding.

Humboldt all of a sudden stopped dead.

Now what, called Bonpland, furious.

Humboldt asked if he could see it too.

Of course he could, said Bonpland, who had no idea what Humboldt was talking about.

He had to ask, said Humboldt. He couldn't trust his own senses. The dog kept mixing itself in.

Bonpland said he'd never been able to stand the dog.

This ravine here, said Humboldt, was a real ravine, wasn't it?

Bonpland looked down. In front of their feet a crack opened a good four hundred feet down into the deep. The track continued on the other side and the peak didn't seem to be that much further.

They would never manage to cross!

Bonpland had a shock, because he wasn't the one who'd spoken, it was the man to his right. But to be sure of its validity, he said it again himself. They would never manage to cross!

Never, said the man to his left. Unless they could fly.

Slowly, as if pushing against some resistance, Humboldt knelt and opened the container with the barometer. His hands were trembling so hard that he almost dropped it. Blood was running from his nose

170

now too and dripping down onto his coat. No mistakes now, he said imploringly.

Gladly, said Bonpland.

Somehow Humboldt managed to light a fire and heat a little pot of water. He couldn't rely on the barometer, he explained, and not on his brain either, he had to calculate their altitude by establishing the boiling point. His eyes were narrowed and his lips trembled with the effort of concentration. When the water boiled, he measured the temperature and read off the clock. Then he pulled out his writing pad. He crumpled half a dozen sheets before his hand obeyed him sufficiently to allow him to write numbers.

Bonpland stared mistrustfully down into the ravine. The sky hung there far below them, rough-coated in frost. It seemed possible to adapt somewhat to standing on your head. But not to Humboldt taking so long to do his sums. Bonpland asked if they'd have the answer today.

Please excuse him, said Humboldt, he was having difficulty pulling himself together. Please could someone put the dog on the lead!

He'd never been able to stand the dog, said Bonpland. And then immediately was ashamed because he'd said it already. He was so embarrassed that he felt sick. He bent forward and vomited again.

Finished, asked Humboldt. Then he could tell him that they were now at an altitude of eighteen thousand six hundred and ninety feet.

Oh hallelujah, said Bonpland.

This made them the people who had climbed higher than anyone in history. No one had ever gone so far above sea level.

But the summit?

With or without the summit, it was a world record.

He wanted to get to the summit, said Bonpland.

Didn't he see the ravine, screamed Humboldt. They were neither of them in their right minds any more. If they didn't start down now, they'd never return at all.

One could always, said Bonpland, just say one had been up to the top.

Humboldt said he didn't want to have heard that.

He hadn't said it. It was the other one who'd said it.

Nobody could check, said Humboldt thoughtfully.

Quite, said Bonpland.

He hadn't said that, cried Humboldt.

Said what, said Bonpland.

They stared at each other, baffled.

The altitude had been established, said Humboldt finally. And the rock samples gathered. Now down, as fast as possible!

The descent took a long time. They had to make a wide detour round the ravine they had crossed on the snow bridge. But they had a clear view now, and Humboldt had no difficulty finding the path. Bonpland stumbled after him. His knees felt treacherous. He kept having the sensation that he was walking in running water, and an optical refraction displaced his legs in a most difficult way. And the stick in his hand was misbehaving: it swung outward, stabbed itself into the snow, tapped against fragments of rock, without

172

Bonpland being able to do anything except follow it. The sun was already low. Humboldt slid down a scree slope. His hands and face were scraped bloody, and his coat torn, but the barometer didn't break.

Pain had its uses, he said through clenched teeth. For the moment, he could see clearly again. The dog had vanished.

He'd never been able to stand the dog, said Bonpland.

They had to make it down today, said Humboldt. The night would turn cold. They were confused. They wouldn't survive. He spat blood. He was sorry about the dog. He had loved it.

Since they were being candid right now, said Bonpland, and tomorrow everything could be blamed on altitude sickness, he wanted to know what Humboldt had been thinking up there on the snow bridge.

He had ordered himself not to think, said Humboldt. And so he hadn't thought anything.

Really nothing at all?

Absolutely nothing.

Bonpland blinked in the direction of the slowly fading honeycomb. Two of his companions were gone. He still had one to get rid of. But perhaps that wasn't even necessary. He had the suspicion that it might be himself.

The two of them, said Humboldt, had climbed the highest mountain in the world. That would remain a fact, whatever else happened in their lives.

Not all the way, said Bonpland.

Rubbish!

A person who climbed a mountain reached the peak. A person who didn't reach the peak hadn't climbed the mountain.

Humboldt stared at his bleeding hands and said nothing.

Up there on the bridge, said Bonpland, he had suddenly regretted that he had to go second.

That was only human, said Humboldt.

Not just because the one who went first would reach safety earlier. He had had strange fantasies. If he had been going first, something inside him would have liked to give the bridge a kick as soon as he was over on the other side. The wish had been strong.

Humboldt didn't reply. He seemed to be sunk in his own thoughts.

Bonpland's head hurt, and he felt feverish again. He was deadly tired. It would be a long time before he recovered from today. A man who traveled far, he said, learned many things. Some of them about himself.

Humboldt begged his pardon. Unfortunately he hadn't understood a word. The wind!

Bonpland said nothing for several seconds. Nothing important, he said, thankfully. Chatter. Just talk.

Well then, said Humboldt expressionlessly. No reason to dawdle!

Two hours later they came upon their waiting guides. Humboldt demanded the return of his letter and immediately tore it up. One could not be neglectful about these things. Nothing was more embarrassing than a farewell letter whose writer was still alive.

He didn't care, said Bonpland, holding his pounding head. They could keep his or throw it away. They could also send it if they wanted.

That night, huddled under a blanket against the driving snow, Humboldt wrote two dozen letters, in which he made Europe party to the news that he had climbed higher than any mortal who had ever existed. Carefully he sealed each one. Only then did he lose consciousness.

The Garden

Late in the evening, the professor knocked at the door of the manor house. A thin young servant opened up and said that Count von der Ohe zur Ohe was not receiving.

Gauss asked him to repeat the name.

The servant did so: Count Hinrich von der Ohe zur Ohe.

Gauss had to laugh.

The servant looked at him as if he'd stepped in a cowpat. The gracious gentleman's family had borne this name for a thousand years.

Germany was a funny little place, said Gauss. However, he was here to do the land survey. All obstacles were to be removed. The state must recompense Herr . . . He smiled. The state was obliged to buy several trees and a worthless shed from the count. A formality, it wouldn't take long.

That might be possible, said the servant. But not this evening.

Gauss looked down at his dirty shoes. He had feared as much. Good, then he would have to spend the night here, please prepare a room for him.

He didn't think there was room, said the servant.

Gauss removed his velvet cap, mopped his forehead, and fingered his collar. He felt sweaty and not very well. His stomach hurt. There must be a misunderstanding. He wasn't here as a supplicant. He was the head of the State Boundaries Commission and if he was turned away, when he came back he would have people with him. Was he making himself clear?

The servant took a step back.

Was he making himself clear?

Yes indeed, said the servant.

Yes indeed, Herr Professor!

Herr Professor, the servant said after him.

And now he wished to see the count.

The servant frowned so hard that his entire brow crumpled. He must have failed to make himself clear. The gracious gentleman had already retired. He was asleep!

Only for a moment, said Gauss.

The servant shook his head.

Sleep was not a fate. A sleeping man could be woken. The longer he had to stand here, the later it would be before the count got back to his featherbed, and his own mood would not be improving either. He was dog-tired.

Hoarsely, the servant commanded him to follow him.

He advanced so quickly with the candleholder that he seemed to be hoping he could run from Gauss. It would not have been hard: Gauss's feet hurt, the leather of his shoes was too stiff, the skin under his woolen shirt itched, and a searing sensation in his neck told him that he had got sunburn again. They went down a low corridor with faded tapestries. A maid with a pretty figure went past carrying a chamber pot, and Gauss looked after her longingly. They went down a flight of stairs, then up again, then down again. The layout must be intended to be confusing to visitors, and presumably succeeded in doing just that to people who lacked a sense of geometrical projection. Gauss estimated that they were now approximately twelve feet above and forty feet west of the front door, and were moving in a southwesterly direction. The servant knocked at a door, opened it, addressed a few words to the interior, and let Gauss enter. An old man in a dressing gown and wooden slippers was sitting in a rocking chair. He was tall, with hollow cheeks and piercing eyes.

Von der Ohe zur Ohe, a pleasure. What are you laughing at?

He wasn't laughing, said Gauss. He was the state land surveyor. He never laughed, and had merely wished to introduce himself and express his thanks for the hospitality.

The count asked if that was why he had been woken.

Precisely, said Gauss. And now he wished him a good night! Satisfied, he followed the servant down another staircase and along a particularly stuffy corridor. These people would never again treat him like a domestic!

His triumph didn't last long. The servant brought him to an appalling hole. It stank, the floor was scattered with rotting hay, the bed was a wooden plank, and the washing arrangements consisted of a rusty bucket of unclean water. No toilet to be seen.

He had already had quite some experiences, said Gauss. Two weeks ago a farmer had offered him a kennel. But that had been better than this.

That could be, said the servant, as he left. But this was all there was.

Groaning, Gauss made himself lie down on the plank bed. The pillow was hard and smelled bad. He put his cap on top, but that didn't help. For a long time sleep eluded him. His back hurt, the air was foul, he was afraid there might be ghosts, and as he did every evening, he missed Johanna. Fail to pay attention for a single moment and there you were with an official job, traipsing through the woods, and negotiating with farmers about their lopsided trees. Just this afternoon he had paid five times what it was worth for an old birch tree. It had taken forever for his assistants to saw through the obstinate trunk so that he could take bearings from Eugen's light signals with the theodolite. And of course the ass had begun by blinking in the wrong direction! Tomorrow they would meet up and he would have to work out how to get to the next junction in two straight lines maximum. This was now his profession. The book on astronomy was long since published, and he was on leave from the university. Nonetheless the work was well paid, and with a little ingenuity it was possible in various ways to earn a little extra on the side. With these thoughts he went to sleep.

Early in the morning he was awoken by a tormenting dream. He saw himself lying on the plank bed and dreaming that he was lying on the plank bed dreaming that he was lying on the plank bed and dreaming. Uneasily he sat up and realized immediately that he wasn't yet awake. Then he started switching realities from one second to the next, and then again, and none of them had anything better to offer than the same filthy room with hay on the floor and a bucket of water in the corner. Once there was a tall, shadowed figure standing in the door, and another time a dog lay dead in the corner, then a child in a wooden mask came wandering in by mistake, but before he could see it clearly, it was gone again. When finally he sat exhausted on the edge of the bed and looked up into the sunny morning sky, he couldn't shake the feeling that he had almost lost touch with the reality in which he really belonged. He splashed cold water on his face and thought of Eugen, whom he would meet that afternoon. Usually it improved his mood to be able to scream at him. He got dressed and went out yawning.

He walked through suites of rooms with paintings to which time had not been kind: earnest men, badly painted, the colors applied too thickly. Stained wooden furniture, dust everywhere. He paused in front of a mirror, and thought. He didn't like what he saw. He opened some drawers, but they were empty. He was relieved to find an iron-barred door into the garden.

This was laid out with astonishing care: palm trees, orchids, orange trees, bizarrely shaped cacti, and every variety of plant, ones Gauss had never even seen in pictures. Gravel crunched under his shoes and a liana brushed the cap from his head. It smelled of something sweet, and burst fruit lay scattered on the ground. The growth became thicker, the path narrowed, and he had to bend over as he walked. The prodigality! He could only hope that the place didn't have strange insects too. As he pushed his way between the trunks of two palms, his jacket got caught and he almost stumbled into a thorn bush. Then he was standing in a meadow. In an armchair, still in his nightshirt, hair every which way and feet bare, the count was sitting drinking tea.

Impressive, said Gauss.

In the old days it was much more beautiful, said the count. Gardening staff were expensive now, and the French occupation had destroyed a great deal. He'd only recently returned here. He had been in Switzerland, an émigré, and now things had changed for the moment. Would the surveyor not care to be seated?

Gauss looked around. There was only one chair, and the count was sitting in it. Not particularly, he said hesitantly.

Yes, so now, said the count. One could have the negotiations.

A mere formality, said Gauss. In order to have a clear view of the measuring point at Scharnhorst, he would have to fell three trees in the count's wood and tear down a shed that had obviously been standing empty for years.

Scharnhorst? Nobody could see that far!

Yes they could, said Gauss, provided they used concentrated light. He had developed an instrument which could send light signals over unimaginable distances. For the first time it made it possible to have communication between earth and sun.

Earth and sun, repeated the count.

Gauss smiled and nodded. He could see exactly what was going on in the old idiot's head now.

As for trees and shed, said the count, it was a question of compensation. The shed was essential. The trees were valuable.

Gauss sighed. He would have liked to sit down. How many of these conversations had he now had to have? Of course, he said wearily, but one shouldn't exaggerate. He knew perfectly well what some wood and a hut were worth. Right now in particular was no time to burden the state unreasonably.

Patriotism, said the count. Interesting. Particularly when it was being demanded by someone who had been a French official until very recently.

Gauss stared at him.

The count sipped his tea and asked him not to misunderstand him. He wasn't reproaching anyone. Times had been bad, and everyone had behaved according to his own possibilities.

On his account, said Gauss, Napoleon had refrained from bombarding Göttingen!

The count nodded. He didn't seem surprised. Not everyone had had the luck to be esteemed by the Corsican.

And almost no one had earned it either, said Gauss.

The count looked dreamily into his cup. It would seem that the surveyor was not as inexperienced in business dealings as he pretended.

Gauss asked how he should interpret this.

He was right, was he not, to assume that the surveyor would pay him in the usual coin of the realm?

Of course, said Gauss.

Then he must ask himself if these expenses of the state would not be reimbursed to the surveyor in gold. If this were indeed the case, there must be a pretty gain to be made from the exchange rate. One didn't have to be a mathematician to see it.

Gauss went red.

At least not the so-called Prince of Mathematicians, said the count, who could hardly fail to notice such a thing.

Gauss clasped his hands behind his back and looked at the orchids growing on the palm trees. None of it was against the law, he said tightly.

No doubt, said the count. He was sure the surveyor had verified this. Moreover he had a great admiration for the art of surveying. It was a peculiar activity, traveling around with instruments for months at a time.

Only in Germany. Do the same thing in the Cordilleras and you would be celebrated as a discoverer.

The count shook his head. It must be hard, all the same, particularly if one had a family at home. The surveyor had a family, yes? A good wife?

Gauss nodded. The sun seemed too bright and the plants were making him uneasy. He asked if they could discuss the sale of the trees. He had to move on, his time was very limited.

Not so very limited, said the count. If one had written the *Disquisitiones Arithmeticae*, one must presumably never have to hurry again.

Gauss looked at the count in astonishment.

Please, no unnecessary modesty, said the count. The section on dividing the circle was one of the most remarkable things he had ever read. He had found thoughts in it that even he had been able to learn from.

Gauss laughed out loud.

Yes, yes, said the count, he really meant it.

He was astonished, said Gauss, to meet a man with such interests here.

He would do better to speak of knowledge, said the count. His interests were very limited. But he had always considered it necessary to extend his knowledge beyond the limits of his interests. By the way, he had heard that the surveyor wished to say something to him.

Pardon?

It was some time ago. Burdens, annoyances. Even a formal complaint.

Gauss rubbed his forehead. He was beginning to feel hot, and he had no idea what this man was talking about.

Really not?

Gauss looked at him blankly.

Then not, said the count. And as for the trees, he would donate them for nothing.

And the shed?

That too.

But why, asked Gauss, and was shocked at himself. What a stupid mistake!

Did one always need reasons? For love of the state, as was suitable for a citizen. As a gesture of his esteem for the surveyor.

Gauss thanked him with a bow. He must leave now, his useless son was waiting, he had the long walk to Kalbsloh ahead of him.

The count returned the salutation with a fluttering gesture of his thin hand.

On the way to the manor house, Gauss thought for a moment that he was disoriented. He concentrated, then went right, left, right again, through the iron-barred door, then right again twice, through another door, and was in the entrance hall from the day before. The servant was already waiting, opened the front door, and apologized for the room. He hadn't known whom he was dealing with. That had just been the room for passing travelers where they lodged riffraff and vagabonds. It was not at all bad upstairs. There were mirrors and washbasins and even bedclothes.

Riffraff and vagabonds, Gauss echoed.

Yes, said the servant expressionlessly. Scum and lowlife. And he shut the door gently.

Gauss took a deep breath. He was relieved to be out of there. He had to get away at once, before the madman regretted having given his consent. So he'd read the *Disquisitiones*! He had never become accustomed to being famous. Even back then, at the worst point of the war, when an adjutant had arrived bringing greetings from Napoleon, he had thought

185

there was some misunderstanding. And indeed perhaps there had been; he would never know. He strode quickly from the slope into the wood.

In the most irritating fashion, the trees he had marked yesterday were in perfect hiding. It was sultry, he was sweating, and there were too many flies. Every tree that had to go had been marked with a cross in chalk. Now he had to put another one on them, as a sign that he had permission to have them felled. Eugen had asked recently if it didn't upset him, the trees were so old and tall, and they gave such generous shade. The boy was as sensitive as he was slow. A tragedy: he had been so determined to nourish the gifts of his children, to make learning easy for them, and to call out everything in them that was exceptional. But then there had been nothing exceptional to call out. They were not even particularly intelligent. Joseph was making good as an officer candidate, but he took after Johanna. Wilhelmine was admittedly obedient and kept the house clean. But Eugen?

Eventually he found the shed and was able to mark it too. It would probably be days before his assistants tore it down. Then he would be able to specify the angle against the baseline, and the net would be larger by one more triangle. That was how he must work his way up, step by step, all the way to the Danish border.

Soon all this would be trivial. People would go up in balloons and measure off distances on magnetic scales. They would send galvanic signals from one measuring point to the next and work out distances by the diminution of electrical intensity. But none of this helped him now, he had to do it with a measuring tape and theodolite in muddy boots, and also work out methods using pure mathematics to balance out inaccuracies of measurement: tiny errors added up every time to a catastrophe. There had never been an accurate map of this region or any other.

His nose itched; a gnat had bitten him. He wiped away the sweat. He thought of Humboldt's report on the mosquitoes of the Orinoco: humans and insects couldn't coexist over the long haul, not forever, not for all time. Just last week Eugen had been stung by a hornet. Presumably there must be a million insects for every human being. Even with great luck and skill, one couldn't exterminate them all. He sat down on a tree stump, pulled a hard crust of bread from his pocket, and bit into it cautiously. Seconds later the first wasps were buzzing round his head. Looking at it soberly, one had to assume the insects would win.

He thought about his wife Minna. He had never lied to her. First he had considered marrying Nina, but Bartels had convinced him in a long letter that he was not permitted to do that. So he had explained to Minna that he needed someone for the children, and for the housekeeping, and his mother, that he couldn't live alone, and besides she had been Johanna's best friend. Her engagement with some idiot had recently been broken off, she wasn't young any more, her chances of marrying weren't good. She had giggled in shame, left the room, come back in again, and pulled at her dress. Then she had cried a little and accepted. He thought of their wedding, of the fright it had given him to see her in white, her big teeth bared in a happy smile. That was when he recognized his mistake. The problem wasn't that he didn't love her. The problem was that he couldn't stand her. That her presence made him nervous and unhappy, that her voice sounded like a piece of chalk on a blackboard, that even the sight of her face in the distance made him feel lonely, and the very thought of her was enough to make him wish he were dead. Why had he become a land surveyor? To get away from home.

He noticed that he had lost his sense of direction again. He looked up. The treetops soared into a hazy sky. The forest floor under his feet was springy. He must be careful, one could easily slip and fall on the damp roots. He would have to find lunch with a farmer, and as always he would get stomach cramps from the bread soup and the fat milk. And every doctor in the country said that sweating wasn't healthy.

Hours later, Eugen found him wandering in the woods, cursing.

Why not till now, roared Gauss.

Eugen swore that he couldn't help being late, a farmer had sent him in the wrong direction, then he had missed the marking on the hut, it was too small, and a goat had been lying right in front. When he did notice the cross mark, the animal had attacked him. He had never been bitten by a goat before. He didn't know such a thing could happen.

Gauss sighed and stretched out his hand; expecting a slap on the ears, the boy flinched away. He had only intended to pat him on the shoulder. Anger rose up in

Gauss; now he could no longer complete the gesture without embarrassing himself. So he had to give him a slap on the cheek. It landed a little too hard, and Eugen stared at him wide-eyed.

Why are you slouching there like that, said Gauss to justify the blow. Stand up straight! He took the heliotrope Eugen had collected from his hands. No doubt about it, the boy had Minna's intelligence and from his father only a tendency to melancholy. Gauss gently stroked the crystal mirror, the scales, and the swiveling telescope. People would use this invention for a long time! He wished, he said, that he could have demonstrated the instrument to the count.

What count?

Gauss groaned. Since childhood, he had had to accustom himself to other people's slowness. But he could not permit it in his own son. Stupid donkey, he said, and started walking. The very thought of how much there still was to do made him dizzy. Germany was not an urbanized country, it was peopled by farmers and a few eccentric aristocrats, and it consisted of thousands of woods and little villages. He felt he was going to have to visit every one of them.

The Capital

In New Spain, the first reporter was waiting.

They had almost not made it that far, because the captain of the only ship to Acapulco had refused to allow foreigners on board. Passports were neither here nor there, he was from New Granada, Spain didn't interest him, and Urquijo's seal was meaningless, here in any case and now back there as well. Humboldt hadn't wanted to pay bribes out of principle; eventually they solved it by Humboldt giving the money to Bonpland and Bonpland slipping it to the captain.

On the way, the volcano Cotopaxi had erupted, setting off a storm, and because the captain had ignored Humboldt's advice — he'd been doing this run for years, and it was going against the law of the sea to criticize your navigator, members of his crew could get hanged for doing that — they were driven way off-course. So that the storm wouldn't be useless, Humboldt had himself tied to the bow fifteen feet above the water, to measure the height of the waves out clear of the coast. He had hung there for a whole day, from first light until nightfall, the eyepiece of the sextant held to his face. Admittedly he was a little confused after it was over, but also all red, refreshed, and full of good cheer, and had been unable to grasp why the sailors took him for the Devil after that.

So — a man with a big mustache was standing at the gangway when they reached Acapulco. He introduced himself as Gómez, writing for numerous journals both in New Spain and in the mother country. He asked, humbly, if he might accompany the count.

Not count, said Bonpland. Merely baron.

Since he wished to write up his journey himself, this struck him as unnecessary, said Humboldt, casting a reproachful look at Bonpland.

Gómez promised he would be a shadow, a ghost, effectively invisible, but that he wanted to witness everything that needed witnesses.

Humboldt first of all established the geographical position of the capital. An exact atlas of New Spain, he dictated to Gómez as he lay on his back and aimed his telescope at the night sky, could encourage the settlement of the colonies, hasten the conquest of nature, and steer the fate of the country in a favorable direction. Apparently a German astronomer had calculated the path of a new wandering planetoid. Unfortunately it was impossible to know in exact detail, journals here were late in arriving. Sometimes he wished he were home. He lowered the telescope and asked Gómez to strike the last two sentences from his notes.

They headed into the mountains. Bonpland had recovered from his fever: he looked thinner, and pale despite the sun, and he had his first wrinkles and noticeably less hair than a few years before. A new thing was that he chewed his fingernails and coughed from time to time out of sheer habit. He was missing so many teeth now that eating was hard for him.

Humboldt, by contrast, seemed unchanged. With his old industriousness he was working on a topographic map of the continent. He drew in the vegetation zones, the incremental drop in air pressure, the layering of rock inside the mountain ranges. To distinguish between the stone formations, he crawled into holes in the rock so small that he got stuck more than once and Bonpland had to haul him out by the feet. He climbed a tree, a branch broke, and Humboldt fell on top of Gómez as he busily took notes.

Gómez asked Bonpland what kind of a person Humboldt was.

He knew him better than anyone, said Bonpland. Better than he knew his mother and father, better even than he knew himself. He hadn't sought this out, but that's the way it had happened.

And?

Bonpland sighed. He had absolutely no idea.

Gómez asked how long they'd been traveling together.

He didn't know, said Bonpland. Maybe a lifetime. Maybe longer.

Why had he taken all this on?

Bonpland looked at him with bloodshot eyes.

Why, repeated Gómez, had he taken all this on? Why was he the assistant —

Not the assistant, said Bonpland, the collaborator.

So why had he remained this man's collaborator through all their trails, for years on end?

Bonpland thought. Lots of reasons.

For example?

Well, said Bonpland, he'd simply always wanted to get away from La Rochelle. Then one thing had led to another. Time went by so ridiculously fast.

That, said Gómez, wasn't an answer.

He had to dissect cacti now. Bonpland turned away and briskly clambered up the little hill.

Meanwhile Humboldt was climbing down into the mine at Taxco. He spent some days observing the silver extraction, inspected the timber casings for the tunnels, hammered stone, and talked to the foremen. With his breathing mask and miner's lamp he looked demonic. Wherever he turned up, workers fell to their knees and begged God to help them. More than once the foremen had to shield him when stones were thrown.

The thing that fascinated him most was the workers' genius for thievery. No one was allowed into the mine bucket before being completely searched. Nonetheless they always found ways to take clumps of earth with them. Humboldt asked if for reasons of scientific research he might take part in the body searches. He found lumps of silver in the men's hair, their armpits, their mouths, even their anuses. This kind of work was repugnant to him, he said to the mine superintendent, one Don Fernando García Utilla, who was watching him in a kind of dreamy state as he felt around a little boy's navel; but science and the welfare of the state required it. An orderly exploitation of the earth's deep treasures wasn't possible if one didn't counteract the selfish interests of the workers. He said the sentence again so that Gómez could keep up. Moreover it would be advisable to do some repairs on the mine itself. There were too many accidents.

They had enough people, said Don Fernando. Anyone who died could be replaced.

Humboldt asked if he'd read Kant.

A little, said Don Fernando. But he'd had his objections. He preferred Leibniz. He came of German stock, which was how he knew all these wonderful mad ideas.

The day of their departure there were two captive balloons stationary in the sky, round and shining in the sun. It was the fashion these days, Gómez explained, every man of means and courage wanted to fly at least once.

Years ago he had seen the first balloon over Germany, said Humboldt. It was a lucky man who went up then. When it was no longer God's miracle but before there was anything earthly about it. Like discovering a new star.

At Cuernavaca they were hailed by a young man from North America. He had a wonderfully coiffed beard, his name was Wilson, and he wrote for the *Philadelphia Chronicle*.

It was all getting too much for him, said Humboldt.

Naturally the United States was in the shadow of its mighty neighbor, said Wilson. But even in this young country, the public had a growing fascination with General Humboldt and his deeds.

Mine inspector, said Humboldt, to head off Bonpland. Not general.

Outside the capital, Humboldt put on his grandest dress uniform. A delegation from the viceroy was awaiting them on a hill, bearing the keys to the city. Since Paris they had not set foot in any metropolis on this scale. There was a university, a free library, a botanical garden, an Academy of the Arts, and an Academy of Mines, patterned on the Prussian model and headed by Humboldt's former Freiberg fellow student Andrés del Río. The latter did not seem overjoyed to see him again. He put his hands on Humboldt's shoulders, held him at arm's length, and looked at him through slit eyes.

So it was true, he said in broken German. Despite all the talk.

What talk? Since the meeting with Brombacher, Humboldt hadn't needed his mother tongue. His German sounded wooden and uncertain, and he kept having to search for words.

Rumors, said Andrés. Along the lines that he was a spy for the United States. Or for Spain.

Humboldt laughed. A Spanish spy in the Spanish colonies?

But yes, said Andrés. They would not remain a colony for long. They knew that over there, and here they knew it even better.

Near the main square, excavations had begun on the remains of the temple destroyed by Cortés. Yawning workers stood around in the shadow of the cathedral, and the penetrating smell of tortillas hung in the air.

On the ground were skulls with gems for eyes, dozens of obsidian knives, stones beautifully incised with pictures of human slaughter, and small clay figures with open ribcages. There was also a stone altar made of crudely carved skulls. The smell of maize troubled Humboldt, it made him feel sick. As he turned around he saw Wilson and Gómez with their notepads.

He asked them to leave him alone, he needed to concentrate.

This was how a great scientist worked, said Wilson.

Alone, so that he could concentrate, said Gómez. The world must know this!

Humboldt was standing in front of a gigantic stone wheel. A whirlwind of lizards, snakes' heads, and human figures broken into geometric fragments. In the center, a face with out-stretched tongue and lidless eyes. Slowly the chaos resolved itself; he recognized correspondences, images that enlarged one another, symbols repeated at minutely regulated intervals, and that encoded numbers. It was a calendar. He tried to draw it, but couldn't, and it had something to do with the face at the center. He asked himself where he had seen that look before. He thought of the jaguar, then of the boy in the mud hut. He stared uneasily at his drawing tablet. For this he would need a professional artist. He stared into the face, and it must have been the heat or the smell of maize that made him suddenly turn away.

Twenty thousand, said a worker in a pleased way. Twenty thousand people were sacrificed when the temple was dedicated. One after the other: heart out, head off. The rows of waiting victims had stretched all the way to the boundaries of the city.

My good man, said Humboldt, don't talk nonsense!

The worker looked at him, insulted.

Twenty thousand in one place, in one day, was unthinkable. The victims would never tolerate it. The audience wouldn't tolerate it. What was more, the world order would not support it. If such a thing ever happened, the universe would come to an end.

The universe, said the worker, didn't give a shit.

In the evening, Humboldt dined with the viceroy. Andrés del Río and several members of the government were there, a museum director, some officers, and a small taciturn man with dark skin and unusually elegant clothes: the conde of Moctezuma, great-grandson of the last god-king and grandee of the Spanish Empire. He lived in a castle in Castile and had business in the colony for a few months. His wife, a tall beauty, looked at Humboldt with undisguised interest.

Twenty thousand was indeed correct, said the viceroy. Perhaps even more, calculations differed. Under Tlacaelel, the last high priest, the kingdom had become addicted to blood.

Not that the office of high priest was that desirable, said Andrés. Priests were obliged to mutilate themselves on a regular basis. For example, he begged the ladies' pardon, on important feast days they let blood from their own genitals.

Humboldt cleared his throat and began to talk about Goethe, and also his elder brother, and their common interest in the languages of ancient peoples. They considered them to be a finer form of Latin, more pure, and closer to the origin of the world. He wondered if this might also be true of the Aztec language.

The viceroy looked questioningly at the conde.

He could not provide any such information, said the latter without looking up from his plate. He spoke only Spanish.

To change the subject, the viceroy asked Humboldt's opinion of the silver mines.

Ineffective, said Humboldt absentmindedly, nothing but dilettantism and shoddy work. He closed his eyes for a moment, and immediately the stone face appeared in front of him. Something had seen him, he could feel it, and would never forget him. Only the enormous surplus of silver, he heard himself saying, allowed an appearance of efficiency. The methods were antiquated, the theft quotient was gigantic, and the personnel were undereducated.

For a few moments there was silence. The viceroy threw a glance at Andrés del Río, who had turned pale.

Of course he was exaggerating, said Humboldt, shocked at himself. A lot of things had impressed him!

The conde looked at him with a faint smile.

New Spain needed a capable minister of mines, said the viceroy.

Humboldt asked whom he had in mind.

The viceroy said nothing.

Impossible, said Humboldt, raising his hands. He was a Prussian, he could not serve another country.

Only later in the evening did he manage to exchange a few words with the conde. He asked him quietly what he might know about an enormous stone calendar-wheel.

About five ells in radius?

Humboldt nodded.

With feathered snakes, and a staring face at the center?

Yes, cried Humboldt.

He didn't know a thing, said the conde. He wasn't an Indian, he was a Spanish grandee.

Humboldt enquired if nothing was passed down in the family.

The conde drew himself up to his full height, level with Humboldt's chest. His forefather had been kidnapped by Cortés. He had begged for his life like a woman, had moaned and wept and finally, after weeks of imprisonment, had changed sides. It was Aztecs who had stoned him to death. If he, the conde of Moctezuma, were to walk out now into the main square, he wouldn't stay alive for five minutes. The conde paused for thought. Perhaps, he said finally, nothing might happen at all. It had all been a long time ago, people scarcely remembered any more. He took his wife by the elbow and looked up at Humboldt with narrowed eyes. Everyone who met him searched his face for a glimpse of the god-king. Everyone who heard his name looked through him and into the past. Could Humboldt imagine what it was like to lead one's life as the shadow of a great relative?

Sometimes, yes, said Humboldt.

Passed down in the family, the conde repeated disapprovingly. He and his wife left without saying goodbye.

In the early morning, Humboldt noticed that Bonpland wasn't there. He immediately went in search of him. The streets were full of traders: one man was selling dried fruit, a second miraculous cures for every illness except arthritis, a third struck off his left hand with an axe, then handed it round for the crowd to examine while he waited in pain until he got it back again. He pressed it against the stump and dripped a tincture over it. Pale from loss of blood, he then banged on the table to show it had reattached itself. The bystanders applauded and bought his entire stock of tincture. A fourth had a miraculous cure for arthritis, a fifth cheaply printed illustrated brochures. One of them contained the story of a miracle-working priest, another the life of the Indian boy to whom the Madonna of Guadeloupe had appeared, a third the adventure of a German baron, who had steered a boat through the hell of the Orinoco and climbed the highest mountain in the world. The pictures were really not bad; Humboldt's uniform in particular was well captured.

He found Bonpland where he thought he might be. The house was expensively decorated, the façade covered with Chinese tiles. A porter asked him to wait. Minutes later Bonpland appeared, his clothes thrown on in haste.

Humboldt asked how often he would have to remind him of their bargain.

It was a hotel like any other, Bonpland replied, and their bargain was unreasonable. He had never agreed to it.

One way or the other, said Humboldt, it was still a bargain.

Bonpland told him to spare himself the homilies.

Next day they climbed Popocatepetl. A path led almost the entire way to the summit: Gómez and Wilson, the mayor of the capital, three draftsmen, and almost a hundred sightseers followed them. Whenever Bonpland cut off a plant, he had to show it around. Most of them came back so manhandled that there was no point in putting them in the specimen box. When Humboldt put on his breathing mask in front of a hole in the ground, there was applause. And while he established the height of the summit with the barometer and let his thermometer down into the crater, traders sold refreshments.

On the way down they were addressed by a Frenchman. His name, he said, was Duprés and he wrote for several newspapers in Paris. He had come because of the Academy's expedition led by Baudin. But now Baudin hadn't appeared and he hadn't been able to believe his luck when he'd learned that someone infinitely more important was in the country.

For a moment Humboldt was unable to suppress a self-satisfied smile. He still hoped, he said, he might join up with Baudin and go with him to the Philippines. He intended to catch the captain in Acapulco, so that the two of them could explore the blessed islands.

201

The two of them, repeated Duprés. The blessed exploration of the islands.

The exploration of the blessed islands!

Duprés crossed it out, rewrote it, and said thank you.

Then they visited the ruins of Teotihuacán. They seemed too large to have been built by man. A straight highway led them to a square surrounded by temples. Humboldt sat down on the ground to do some calculations, the crowd watched him from a distance. Soon one of them got bored, several of them began to curse, after an hour most of them had gone, after ninety minutes so had the last of them. Only the three journalists remained. Bonpland, covered in sweat, came back from the peak of the largest pyramid.

He hadn't imagined it was so high!

Humboldt, sextant in hand, nodded.

Four hours later, evening was already well advanced, he was still sitting there in the same position, hunched over the paper; Bonpland and the journalists, freezing cold, had dropped off to sleep. Shortly afterward, as Humboldt packed up his instruments, he knew that on the day of the solstice, the sun when seen from the highway rose exactly over the top of the largest pyramid and went down over the top of the second-largest. The whole city was a calendar. Who had thought it up? How well had these people known the stars, and what had they wanted to convey? He was the first person in more than a thousand years who could read their message.

Why was he so depressed, asked Bonpland, awakened by the sound of the instruments being closed.

So much civilization and so much horror, said Humboldt. What a combination! The exact opposite of everything that Germany stood for.

Maybe it was time to go home, said Bonpland.

To the city?

Not this one.

For a while Humboldt stared up into the starry night sky. Good, he said eventually. He would learn to understand these terrifyingly intelligently arranged stones, as if they were natural phenomena. After that he would let Baudin leave on his own for the Pacific and take the first ship to North America. From there they would go back to Europe.

But first they went to Jorullo, the volcano that had suddenly erupted fifty years before in thunder, a storm of fire and a blizzard of ashes. As it appeared in the distance, Humboldt clapped his hands in excitement. He must climb it, he dictated to the journalists, it would provide the final refutation of the theory of Neptunism. When he thought of the great Abraham Werner, he spelled out the name, he almost felt sorry for him.

At the foot of the volcano they were received by the governor of the province of Guanajuato with a great retinue, including the first man to climb it, Don Ramón Espelde. He must insist on leading the expedition. It was too dangerous to be left to laymen!

Humboldt said he had climbed more mountains than anyone else on earth.

Unmoved, Don Ramón advised him not to look directly into the sun and every time he set down his right foot to pray to the Madonna of Guadeloupe.

They dragged along slowly. They kept having to wait for this one or that; Don Ramón in particular kept losing his footing or getting so exhausted he couldn't go on. Humboldt regularly, to universal astonishment, went down on all fours to listen to the rock with his ear-trumpet. Once at the top, he let himself down into the crater on a rope.

The fellow was totally mad, said Don Ramón, he'd never seen anything like it.

When Humboldt was pulled up again he was streaked with green, coughing piteously, and his clothing was scorched. Neptunism, he called out, blinking, was officially buried as of today!

A tragedy really, said Bonpland. It had had a certain poetry.

In Veracruz they took the first ship back to Havana. He had to admit, said Humboldt as the coastline sank away into the haze, he was happy that it was all coming to an end. He leaned against the rail and squinted up into the sky. It occurred to Bonpland that for the first time he didn't look like a young man any more.

They were lucky: in Havana a ship was just leaving to head up the continent, then up the Delaware to Philadelphia. Humboldt went to the captain, showed his Spanish passport one more time, and requested passage.

My God, said the captain, you!

Heavens, said Humboldt.

They stared blankly at each other.

He didn't think it was a good idea, said the captain.

But he had to get north, said Humboldt, and promised not to check any of their positions during the voyage. He trusted him completely. The ocean crossing back then had stayed in his memory as a brilliant feat of seamanship. Despite the disease, the incompetent ship's doctor, and all the false calculations.

And Philadelphia of all places, said the captain. If it were up to him, all rebellious settlers could drop dead, the ones over there and the ones here.

He had fourteen chests full of rock and plant samples, said Humboldt, plus twenty-four cages of monkeys and birds and some glass cases with insects and spiders, which needed special handling. If it was all right, they could begin loading immediately.

This was a busy port, said the captain. Another ship would certainly turn up soon.

He himself would have no objection, said Humboldt. But he had this passport from their Catholic majesties, and they expected him to hurry.

Humboldt kept to his promise and didn't meddle in the navigation. If a monkey hadn't escaped and succeeded on its own in eating half the supplies, loosing two tarantulas, and reducing the captain's cabin to tatters, the voyage would have been without incident. He spent the journey on the afterdeck, sleeping more than usual and writing letters to Goethe, his brother, and Thomas Jefferson. When the chests were unloaded in Philadelphia, the captain and he said another round of farewells.

He very much hoped they would meet again, said Humboldt stiffly.

Certainly no more than he, replied the captain, in his uniform with its scarecrow repairs.

Both saluted.

A coach was waiting to take them into the capital. A messenger delivered a formal invitation: the president asked to have the honor of offering them hospitality in the newly built government residence; he was most eager to learn everything and then more about Herr von Humboldt's already legendary journey.

Uplifting, said Duprés.

Too feeble a word, said Wilson. Humboldt and Jefferson! And he was going to be there too!

And just how was it Herr von Humboldt's journey, asked Bonpland. Why not the Humboldt-Bonpland journey? Or the Bonpland-Humboldt journey? The Bonpland expedition? Could somebody explain it to him just once?

A backwoods president, said Humboldt. Who cared what he thought!

The city of Washington was a building site. Everywhere was covered in scaffolding, trenches, and mounds of bricks, everywhere was a cacophony of saws and hammers. The government residence, just completed and not yet fully painted, was a classical domed building surrounded by columns. He was pleased, said Humboldt as they climbed out of the coach, to see yet another example of the influence of the great Winckelmann!

A double line of raggedy, saluting soldiers had formed up, a trumpet blast cut through the sky, and a flag bellied in the wind. Humboldt held himself ramrod straight and touched the back of his hand to the rim of his cap. Men in dark morning coats were walking down from the building; first came the president, and behind him their foreign minister, Madison. Humboldt said something about the honor of being here, his respect for the liberal idea, and his joy at having left the sphere of an oppressive despotism.

Had he already eaten, asked the president, clapping him on the shoulder. You must eat something, Baron!

The gala dinner was pitiful, but the dignitaries of the republic had all gathered. Humboldt spoke of the ice cold of the Cordilleras and the mosquito swarms of the Orinoco. He was a good narrator, except that he kept losing himself in facts: he reported in such detail on currents and changes of pressure, the relation of elevation to density of vegetation, the minuscule differences between insect species, that several ladies began to yawn. When he took out his notebook and began to read off measurements, Bonpland gave him a kick under the table. Humboldt took a mouthful of wine and moved on to the burden of despotism and the exploitation of earth's riches, which produce a sterile form of wealth from which the economy could never profit. He spoke about the nightmare of slavery. He felt another kick. He cast Bonpland a dirty look and only then realized that it had come from the foreign minister person.

Jefferson had estates, whispered Madison.

And?

With everything that entailed.

Humboldt changed themes. He talked of the squalid harbor of Havana, the highlands of Caxamarca, of Atahualpa's sunken garden of gold, and of the great stone highways, thousands of miles long, built by the Incas to link their countless high redoubts. He had already drunk more than he was accustomed to, his face was flushed and his movements became more expansive. He had always been on the move, ever since he was seven. He had never spent more than six months in one place. He knew every continent and had seen the fabulous creatures described by Oriental fairytales: flying dogs, hydra-headed snakes, and parrots fluent in every language. Then, laughing quietly to himself, he went to bed.

The next day, despite his headache, he had a long conversation in the elliptically formed study of the president. Jefferson leaned back and removed his spectacles.

Bifocal lenses, he explained, exceedingly useful, one of the many inventions of his friend Franklin. Truth be told, the man had always seemed uncanny to him, he had never understood him. Yes, gladly, of course. Here they are!

While Humboldt examined the spectacles, Jefferson folded his hands on his chest and began to ask questions. If Humboldt digressed, he shook his head gently, interrupted, and repeated the question. A map of Central America was lying as if by chance on the table. He wanted to know everything about New Spain, its transport routes and its mines. He was interested in how the administration worked, how orders were transmitted over land and sea, how the mood of the nobles was, how large the army, how well equipped, how well trained. If one had a great power for a neighbor, one could never have enough information. Nonetheless he must alert the baron that since he had been traveling under the auspices of the Spanish crown, he might well be bound to silence.

Oh why, said Humboldt. Who could it hurt? He bent over the map, whose many mistakes he had already pointed out, and put precise crosses on the location of the most important garrisons.

Jefferson sighed and expressed his thanks. What did they know here? They were a tiny Protestant community on the edge of the world. Unimaginably far from everything.

Humboldt glanced through the window. Two workmen were going past carrying a ladder, a third was shoveling out a gravel trench. To be honest, he couldn't wait to go home.

To Berlin?

Humboldt laughed. No one of any intelligence could call that dreadful city home. No, he meant Paris of course. He would never live in Berlin again, of that much he was sure.

The Son

In a bad temper, Gauss laid down his napkin. The food had not been to his taste. But since he was hardly in a position to complain about it, he began to curse the city. He asked how anyone could stand it here.

It had its advantages, said Humboldt vaguely.

Such as?

Humboldt stared at the tabletop for a few moments. He was imagining, he said, covering the earth with a network of magnetic observation points. He wanted to discover whether the planet's interior held one magnet or two, or multiples. The Royal Society had already offered its support, but he still needed the help of the Prince of Mathematicians.

It didn't require a mathematician of any particular skill, said Gauss. He'd already been working on magnetism at the age of fifteen. Child's play. Could he have a cup of tea?

Humboldt snapped his fingers in consternation. It was early afternoon and the professor had been asleep for sixteen hours. Humboldt, on the other hand, had got up at 5a.m. as usual, had gone without breakfast to do a couple of experiments on the fluctuation of the earth's magnetic field, before dictating a memorandum about the costs and possible uses of breeding seals in Warnemünde, writing four letters to two Academies, talking with Daguerre about the apparently insoluble problem of fixing images chemically on copper plates, drinking two cups of coffee, resting for ten minutes, and then proofreading three chapters of the account of his journey with their footnotes about the flora of the Cordillera. He had discussed the order of the upcoming evening reception at the Choral Hall with the secretary of the Society of Natural Scientists, written a short memorandum on the pumping of groundwater for the new Mexican prime minister, and replied to letters of enquiry from two biographers. That was when Gauss, sleep-ridden and grumpy, had appeared from the guest room and demanded breakfast.

As regards Berlin, said Humboldt, he had really had very little choice. After many years in Paris, his circumstances . . . He pushed his white hair back off his face, took out a handkerchief, blew into it gently, folded it, and stroked it smooth before putting it back in his pocket. How should he put it?

The money ran out?

That would be putting it too drastically. But documenting the journey had more or less exhausted his resources. Thirty-four volumes. All the plates and engravings, maps and illustrations. And at a time of war, with material shortages and inflated salaries. He had had to be an Academy all on his own. And so now he was a chamberlain, dined at court, and saw the king daily. There were worse things.

Clearly, said Gauss.

And besides, Friedrich Wilhelm revered science! Napoleon had always hated him and Bonpland because three hundred of his scientists in Egypt had accomplished less than the two of them in South America. After their return they had been the talk of the town for months. Napoleon had found that unacceptable. Duprés had recaptured some very beautiful reminiscences of that time in his *Humboldt — Grand Voyageur*. A book that did less damage to the facts than Wilson's *Scientist and Traveller: My Journeys with Count Humboldt in Central America*.

Eugen asked what had happened to Herr Bonpland. It was clear just by looking at Eugen that he hadn't slept well. He had had to spend the night in the outbuilding in a stuffy room with two of the servants. He hadn't known human beings could snore so loudly.

During his only audience with the emperor, said Humboldt, the latter had asked him if he collected plants. He had said yes, the emperor had said just like his wife and turned away abruptly.

Because of him, said Gauss, Napoleon had chosen not to bombard Göttingen.

So he'd heard, said Humboldt, but he doubted it, it would more likely have been on strategic grounds. But whatever the case, Napoleon had tried later to have him expelled as a Prussian spy. The entire Academy had had to gather to prevent it. And he never — Humboldt threw the secretary a look and the secretary immediately opened his writing pad — he had never wanted to sound out anyone but Nature herself, and

212

the only secrets he had sought were the so openly displayed truths of creation.

The openly displayed truths of creation, the secretary repeated with pursed lips.

The so openly!

The secretary nodded. The servant brought a tray with little silver cups on it.

But Bonpland, Eugen asked again.

A bad business. Humboldt sighed. A really tragic story. But here was the tea finally — a gift from the tsar, whose finance minister had repeatedly invited him to Russia. Naturally he had declined, on political grounds as much — it went without saying — as age.

The right decision, said Eugen. The blackest despotism in the world! He went red with fright over himself.

Gauss bent down, picked up the knobbed stick with a groan, took aim, and struck out under the table at Eugen's foot. He missed and struck again. Eugen jumped.

He couldn't totally disagree, said Humboldt. He made a gesture of dismissal, and the secretary immediately stopped writing. The Restoration lay over Europe like a blight. And he had to admit his brother was partly to blame. The hopes of his youth were a thing of the past and seemed unreal now. On the one side tyranny, on the other the freedom of fools. If three men stood on the street together — he was sure the Gausses knew what he was talking about — it was a forbidden gathering. If thirty of them summoned up spirits in a back room somewhere, nobody had any objections. Dozens of muddled enthusiasts were crisscrossing the country preaching freedom and being fed by unsuspecting fools. Europe was now a theater and the play a nightmare from which none of them could wake any longer. Years ago he had made preparations for a trip to India, had assembled the money, all the equipment, the plan. It should have been the crowning achievement of his earthly life. Then the English had made it impossible. Nobody wanted an enemy of slavery in their territory. And in Latin America dozens of new states had sprung up without rhyme or reason. The life's work of his friend Bolívar now lay in ruins. And did the gentlemen know the title that the Great Deliverer had bestowed on him?

He fell silent. Only after a time did it become clear that he was expecting an answer.

So, what was it, asked Gauss.

The true discoverer of South America! Humboldt smiled into his cup. They could find it in Gómez's *El Barón Humboldt*. An underappreciated book. Apropos, he had heard that the professor was now concentrating on probability theory.

Death statistics, said Gauss. He took a mouthful of tea, made a disgusted face, and set the cup down as far from himself as he could. One thought one controlled one's own existence. One created things, discovered things, acquired goods, found people one loved more than one's life, had children, maybe clever, maybe clods, watched the person one loved die, got old, got ill, and then got buried. One thought one had decided it all oneself. Only mathematics demonstrated that one had always taken the common path. Despotism, he only had to hear the word! Princes were poor pigs too, they lived and struggled and died like everyone else. The real tyrants were the laws of nature.

But it was reason, said Humboldt, that shaped the laws.

The old Kantian nonsense. Gauss shook his head. Reason shaped absolutely nothing and understood very little. Space curved and time was malleable. If one drew a straight line and kept drawing it further and further, eventually one would reencounter its starting point. He pointed to the sun, which hung low in the window. Not even the rays of this dying star came down in straight lines. The world could be calculated after a fashion, but that was a very long way from understanding it.

Humboldt crossed his arms. First of all, the sun would never burn out, it would renew its phlogiston and shine forever. Second of all, what was all that about space? He had had oarsmen in the Orinoco who spun similar nonsense. He had never understood what they were babbling about. But they had often been using substances that confused their minds.

Gauss asked what a chamberlain actually did.

Different things, this and that. This chamberlain in particular advised the king on important decisions, if his experience extended to some field in which it might be of use. He was often asked to be there as adviser during diplomatic conversations. The king desired him to be present at almost every dinner. He was completely obsessed by information about the New World.

So one was paid to eat and have chats?

The secretary sniggered, went pale, and asked pardon, he had a cough.

The real tyrants, said Eugen into the silence, weren't the laws of nature. There were powerful movements afoot in the country, freedom wasn't just a word from the likes of Schiller.

Donkeys' movements, said Gauss.

He had always got on better with Goethe, said Humboldt. Schiller had been closer to his brother.

Donkeys, said Gauss, who would never come to anything. They might inherit some money, and a good name, but never any intelligence.

His brother, said Humboldt, had recently completed a profound study of the works of Schiller. As for himself, literature had never meant that much to him. Books without numbers made him uneasy. And he'd always been bored in the theater.

Quite right, exclaimed Gauss.

Artists were too quick to forget their task, which was to depict reality. Artists held deviation to be a strength, but invention confused people, stylization falsified the world. Take stage sets, which didn't even try to disguise the fact that they were made of cardboard, English paintings, with backgrounds swimming in an oily soup, novels that wandered off into lying fables because the author tied his fake inventions to the names of real historical personages.

Disgusting, said Gauss.

He was working on a catalogue of features of plants and natural phenomena which would be legally obligatory for all painters to consult. Something similar for dramatic poetry would be a good thing. He was thinking of lists of the characteristics of important people, and authors would no longer have the freedom to deviate from them. If Monsieur Daguerre's invention were perfected one day, the arts would become irrelevant anyway.

That one writes poems. Gauss tilted his chin at Eugen.

Really, asked Humboldt.

Eugen went red.

Poems and all kinds of nonsense, said Gauss. Since he was a child. He didn't show them to people, but sometimes he was stupid enough to leave the pieces of paper lying about. He was a miserable scientist, but an even worse artist.

They were being lucky with the weather, said Humboldt. Last month had been extremely wet, but now they could hope for a beautiful fall.

He was a parasite. At least his brother was in the military. But this one hadn't learned anything or had any skills. Poems, if you please!

He was studying rights, said Eugen quietly. And mathematics.

And how, said Gauss. A mathematician who didn't recognize a differential equation until it bit him in the foot. That studying per se didn't amount to anything was common knowledge: he had had to stare at the blank faces of young people for decades. But he'd expected more from his own son. Why did it have to be mathematics?

It wasn't what he'd wanted, said Eugen. He'd been forced!

Oh, and by whom?

The changeable weather and seasons, said Humboldt, were what made the beauty of these latitudes. In contrast to the sheer variety of tropical flora, what Europe offered was the yearly drama of a reawakening creation.

By whom indeed, cried Eugen. And who had employed an assistant for all the measuring?

Magnificent assistance. He had had to remeasure mile upon mile because of all the errors.

Errors in the fifth place after the decimal point! They had absolutely no effect, they were utterly irrelevant.

A moment please, said Humboldt. Errors in measurement were never irrelevant.

And the damaged heliotrope, said Gauss. Was that irrelevant too?

Measuring was a high art, said Humboldt. A responsibility that no one could take lightly.

Two heliotropes, come to that, said Gauss. He'd dropped the other one, but only because some idiot had sent him down the wrong path.

Eugen leapt to his feet, reached for his stick and his red cap, and ran out. The sound of the door banging after him echoed through the castle.

That was what you got, said Gauss. Gratitude was a lost concept.

Of course things weren't easy with the young, said Humboldt. But one also should not be too strict, sometimes a little encouragement was more effective than reproach.

If there was nothing there, nothing would become of it. And as for magnetism, the question as posed was wrong: it wasn't a matter of how many magnets the earth contained. Whichever way you looked at it, there were two poles and a single magnetic field that could be described in terms of the force of the magnetism and the angle of inclination of the needle.

He had always traveled with a magnetic needle, said Humboldt. He had collected more than ten thousand measurements.

God in Heaven, said Gauss. Carrying the thing around wasn't enough, you had to *think*. The horizontal component of magnetic force could be represented as the function of geographical latitude and longitude. The vertical component was best worked out using a power series following the reciprocal earth's radius. Simple functions of a sphere. He laughed softly.

Functions of a sphere. Humboldt smiled. He hadn't understood a single word.

He was out of practice, said Gauss. At twenty he hadn't needed a day for children's stuff like that, now he needed to set aside a week. He tapped his forehead. This up here didn't work the way it once had. He wished he had drunk curare back then. The human brain died a little every day.

One could drink as much curare as one wanted, said Humboldt. One had to drip it into the bloodstream for it to be fatal.

Gauss stared at him. Was that true?

Of course it was true, said Humboldt indignantly. He was the one who'd effectively discovered that.

Gauss was silent for a moment. What, he asked eventually, really did happen to this Bonpland person?

It was time! Humboldt got to his feet. The reception wouldn't wait. After his introductory speech there would be a small reception for the guest of honor. House arrest!

Pardon?

Bonpland was in Paraguay under house arrest. After their return he'd been unable to settle down in Paris. Fame, alcohol, women. His life had lost its clarity and direction, the one thing that must never happen to anybody. For a time he'd been the director of the imperial gardens, and a superb breeder of orchids. After the fall of Napoleon he had gone across the ocean again. He had an estate and a family over there, but he had attached himself to the wrong side in one of the civil wars, or perhaps it was the right one, but in any case it was the losing one. A crazed dictator named Francia, a doctor to boot, had confined him to his estate under permanent threat of death. Not even Simon Bolívar had been able to do anything for Bonpland.

Horrible, said Gauss. But who was the fellow anyway? He'd never heard of him.

220

The Father

Eugen Gauss was wandering through Berlin. A beggar held out an open hand, a dog whimpered at his leg, a hackney horse coughed in his face, and a watchman ordered him not to be ambling about. On a street corner he fell into conversation with a young priest, from the provinces like him, and very intimidated.

Mathematics, said the priest, interesting!

Oh, said Eugen.

His name was Julian, said the priest.

They wished each other well and said goodbye.

A few steps further, a woman addressed him. His knees went weak with fright, for he'd heard of such things. He hurried on, didn't turn round when she ran after him, and never realized that all she had wanted to say to him was that he had dropped his cap. He drank two glasses of beer in a tavern. Arms crossed, he looked at the wet tabletop. He had never felt so sad. Not because of his father, because he was almost always that way, and not because of his loneliness. It was something to do with the city itself. The crowds, the size of the houses, the dirty sky. He composed some lines of poetry. They didn't please him. He stared straight ahead until two students in loose trousers and with fashionably long hair came to sit at his table.

Göttingen, asked one of the students. A notorious place. Things were blowing up there.

Eugen nodded conspiratorially although he had no idea what they were talking about.

But it'll come, said the other student, freedom, in spite of everything.

It would certainly come, said Eugen.

Right away, said the first, and like a thief in the night.

Now they knew they had something in common.

An hour later, they were on the way. As was the custom among students, Eugen went ahead with one of them, arm in arm, while the other followed thirty paces behind, so that they wouldn't be stopped by any gendarme. Eugen couldn't understand how anything could be so far: always more new streets, always another crossroads, and even the sheer numbers of people also walking seemed inexhaustible. Where were they all going, and how could anyone live like that?

Humboldt's new university, explained the student next to Eugen, it was the best in the world, organized like no other and with the most famous teachers in the country. The state feared it like hell itself.

Humboldt had founded a university?

The elder one, the student explained. The respectable one. Not the one who was a lackey of the French and had squatted in Paris for the duration of the war. His brother had openly summoned him to arms, but he'd behaved as if the Fatherland meant nothing. During the occupation, he'd had a plaque put up in front of his castle in Berlin, saying no plundering, the owner was a member of the Paris Academy. Disgraceful!

The street went steeply uphill, then gradually downward again. Two young men stood in front of a door and asked for the password.

Free in the fight.

That was from last time.

The second student came up to them. The two of them whispered together. Germania?

That was ages ago.

German and free?

Oh my God. The guardians exchanged a look, and told them to go in anyway.

They went downstairs and into a cellar room that smelled of mold. Crates stood on the floor and there were wine casks piled in the corners. The two students turned up the lapels of their coats to reveal black and red cockades stitched through with gold. They opened a trapdoor in the floor. A narrow stair led down into another, deeper cellar.

Six rows of chairs in front of a rickety standing desk. Black and red pennants hung on the walls, and about twenty students were already waiting. All had sticks, some were wearing Polish caps, others Old German hats. Several of them were dressed up in home-tailored wide trousers with broad medieval belts. Torches threw dancing shadows on the walls. Eugen sat down, feeling faint from the bad air and the excitement. They were saying, someone whispered, that "he" was coming himself. Him, or someone like him, they didn't know, he had been arrested in Freiburg at the River Unstrut, yet apparently he was still wandering the country incognito. Unimaginable, if he was here in person. Your heart would explode if you saw him in the flesh.

More and more students came in, always in twos, always arm in arm, most of them arguing about the password which clearly none of them had known. Here and there one of them leafed through a book of poetry or *German Gymnastics*. Some moved their lips in prayer. Eugen's heart was thumping. All the seats had been filled long ago, any new arrival had to squeeze himself into a corner.

A man came down the stairs with a heavy tread, and everything went quiet. He was thin, and very tall, with a bald head and a long gray beard. It was, somehow not to Eugen's surprise, their neighbor from the next table in the inn, who had butted into their argument with the gendarme the day before. Slowly, arms swinging, he made his way to the desk. There he stretched, waited until a student, who was having trouble with his trembling hands and had to try more than once, lit the candles on it, and then said in a high-pitched, dry voice: You must not know my name!

Way at the back a student groaned. Otherwise it was completely still.

The bearded man raised his arm, waved it, pointed at it with his other hand, and asked if anyone recognized what this was.

No one answered, no one breathed. So he said it himself: muscles.

You are the brave, he went on after a long pause, you are the young, you are the strong, and you must become stronger still! He cleared his throat. If you want to become thinkers, if you want to read deep, all the way to fundamentals, if you want to touch the very essence of things, you must discipline your bodies. Thinking minus muscles is weakness, it's slack, it's insipid, it's French. A child prays for the Fatherland, a young man is wild for it, but the man fights for it and suffers. He bent over and stayed that way for a moment, before pulling up his trouser leg into regular folds. Here too! He thumped his fist on his calf. Pure and strong, ready to do knee bends or leg extensions, anyone who wanted could come and feel it. He straightened up again and glared around the room for some seconds before thundering: This leg is strong. Germany must be like this leg!

Eugen managed to steal a glance at his neighbors. Several of the audience were gaping, many were in tears, one had closed his eyes and was trembling. His neighbor was chewing his fingers in excitement. Eugen blinked. The air was now even worse and the shadow play of the torches made him think he was part of a far larger crowd. He forced himself to swallow down his own tears.

Nothing must force a comrade to bow, said the bearded man. The enemy must be met face to face, chest to chest. What was oppressing the people was not the strength of the enemy but their own weakness. They were tied and bound. He struck his chest with the flat of his hand. They couldn't breathe, they couldn't move, they didn't know what to do with their own God-given will and brave innocence. Princes, French pests, and priests held them in their power, keeping them coddled and lulled into thumb-sucking sleep. But comradeship meant standing together, pure and devout. It meant thinking! He made a fist and struck his forehead. Thinking would make a holy alliance that no Satan could tear apart. Eventually it would lead to the true German church and the conquest of Being. But what did this mean, comrades? He stretched his arms wide, squatted down slowly, then up again. This signified taking control of the body, schooling it — and up, and down, and climb that rope, and stretch and bend — until one was made whole. But where were things today? Just now, while he was traveling incognito, he had been witness to an old man and a student, a German man and his son, two loyal men, being harassed by the police, because they didn't have papers with them. He had courageously interfered, as a German must, and praise be, he had overwhelmed the tyrant bailiffs. Daily one encountered injustice, of every kind and everywhere, and who should defend against it if not good comrades, who had renounced alcohol and women, and dedicated themselves to strength, Germany's monks, fresh and godly, gay and free? The men of France had been driven out, now it was the princes' turn, the Unholy Alliance would not stand for long, philosophy must seize reality and cudgel a way through, it was time to take command again! He rocked up against the desk and Eugen heard himself and the others cheering. The bearded man stood calmly, very straight, his piercing eyes fixed on the crowd. Suddenly his expression changed, and he took a step back.

Eugen felt a draft. The yelling died away. Five men had walked in: a little old man and four gendarmes.

Good God, said the man next to Eugen. The proctor.

He knew it, said the old man to the gendarmes. All anyone had to do was to watch them all walking around in twos. Luckily they were really that stupid.

Three gendarmes stayed standing in front of the stairs, while one went to the speaker's desk. The bearded man suddenly looked a lot thinner and a lot shorter. He raised a hand over his head, but the threatening gesture had the wrong effect and he was immediately handcuffed.

He wouldn't give way, he cried as the policeman led him to the steps, not to force and not to pleas. His valiant comrades would not permit it. This was the moment when the storm would break. Then, as he was being shoved up the stairs: it was a misunderstanding, he could explain it. Then he was gone.

He was going to fetch reinforcements, said the bailiff, and hurried up the steps.

No talking, said one of the gendarmes. Not a word from anyone to anyone. Otherwise they wouldn't believe what would land on their heads.

Eugen began to cry.

He wasn't the only one. Several young men were sobbing uncontrollably. Two of them who had leapt to their feet sat down again. Fifty students with knobbed sticks, thought Eugen, and three policemen. Only one of them had to attack and the others would follow. And what if it was him? He could do it. For a few seconds he imagined it. Then he knew he was too much of a coward. He wiped his tears away and stayed sitting in silence while the bailiff came back with twenty gendarmes under the command of a big officer with a walrus mustache.

Take them, the officer ordered, first interrogation in the lockup to get the facts, tomorrow hand-over to the competent authorities.

A slight young boy went down on his knees to him, clasped his boots, and begged for leniency. The officer stared at the ceiling, upset and embarrassed, until a gendarme hauled the boy away. Eugen used the moment to tear a page out of his notebook and write the news to his father. Before he was handcuffed he was able to crumple the paper and hide it in his fist.

Police wagons were waiting on the street. The prisoners sat squashed together on long benches with gendarmes standing behind them. By chance Eugen found himself sitting diagonally opposite the bearded man, who was staring dully into space.

Should we make a break for it, whispered a student.

It was a misunderstanding, the bearded man replied, his name was Kösselrieder, he came from Silesia, and he'd stumbled into this. A gendarme hit him on the shoulder with his iron rod and he subsided, muttering quietly to himself.

Anyone else, asked the gendarme.

Nobody moved. The doors shut with a crash and they set off.

The Ether

Eyes half-closed, Humboldt talked of stars and currents. His voice was quiet, but it was audible throughout the reception hall. He stood before the gigantic stage set of a night sky, with stars on it that formed concentric circles: Schinkel's scenery for *The Magic Flute*, re-erected for this occasion. Between the stars someone had inscribed the names of German scientists: Buch, Savigny, Hufeland, Bessel, Klaproth, Humboldt, and Gauss. The hall was filled to the last seat: monocles and spectacles, a myriad of uniforms, softly waving fans, and in the center box, the motionless figures of the crown prince and his wife. Gauss was sitting in the first row.

Oh well, Daguerre whispered good-humoredly into his ear, it would take years before he could take a picture. Certainly the business about getting the exposure right would eventually solve itself, but he and his companion Niepce had no idea how they could fix the silver iodide.

Gauss hissed. Daguerre shrugged his shoulders and lapsed into silence.

Looking into the night sky, said Humboldt, gave no real idea of the sheer extent of this vault. The haze of light surrounding the Magellanic Clouds over the southern hemisphere was not some amorphous substance, some stream or gas; it consisted of suns, and only their absolute distance from earth gave the optical illusion that they all blended into one. A section of the Milky Way, two degrees wide by fifteen degrees long, what could be seen in the eyepiece of a telescope, contained more than fifty thousand countable stars, and up to one hundred thousand if one included those whose weakening light made them impossible to see. Which meant that the Milky Way consisted of twenty million suns, which a human eye that was separated from them by a distance equivalent to their own diameter could only detect as a dull shimmer, one of those patches of mist of which astronomers had counted more than three thousand already. One therefore must ask why, given so many stars, the sky was not permanently filled with light, why there was so much black out there, and one could not avoid accepting the principle that there was something opposed to light, something that acted as a block in the intervening space, a light-extinguishing ether. Once again this gave proof of the rational order of Nature, because finally every human culture began with the observation of the paths of heavenly bodies.

Humboldt opened his eyes wide for the first time. One of these bodies swimming in the black ether was the earth. A kernel of fire, contained in three shells, one rigid, one liquid, and one elastic, all of which offered a home to life. Even deep underground he had found plant matter that grew without light. Volcanoes served

230

earth's fiery core as natural vents, and its rocky crust was covered by two seas, one of water and one of air. Both were moved by perpetual currents: there was the famous Gulf Stream, which drove the water of the Atlantic Ocean past the isthmus of Nicaragua and the Yucatán, then through the Bahama channel northeast against the Newfoundland Banks and from there southeast to the Azores, which explained the miraculous appearance of date palms, flying fish, and sometimes even live Eskimos in their canoes along the Irish coast. He himself had discovered an equally powerful current in the quiet sea that carried cold northern water the length of Chile and Peru to the tropics. Despite all his pleading, he smiled half-proud and half-embarrassed, the sailors insisted on naming it the Humboldt current. It was the same with the currents in the ocean of the air, kept in movement by the fluctuations of the sun's heat, and interrupted by the flanks of the huge stone massifs, which meant that the division of different kinds of plants didn't follow lines of latitude, but rather lines that undulated according to isothermic patterns. This system of currents connected the different parts of earth into a functioning unity. Humboldt was silent for a moment, as if the coming thought moved him. As in earth's caverns, so also in the sea and in the air: plants flourished everywhere. Vegetation was the variousness of life itself, laid out for all to see, silent and immobile. Plants had no interior identity, nothing hidden, everything about them was external. Barely protected, tethered to earth and its dictates, they still managed to live and survive. Insects, by contrast, and animals and humans were both protected and armored. Their constant internal temperature enabled them to tolerate changing conditions. Look at an animal and you didn't know anything; look at a plant and its entire being was laid open to you.

He was getting sentimental, whispered Daguerre.

Life moved up through stages of increasing concealment of its organization until it made the leap that one could confidently name as its final achievement: the lightning bolt of reason. After this there was no further evolution by degrees. The second greatest insult to Man was slavery. But the greatest was the idea that he was descended from the apes!

Man and ape! Daguerre laughed.

Humboldt tilted his head back and seemed to listen to his own words. The understanding of the cosmos had made great strides. Telescopes allowed one to explore the universe, one knew the structure of the earth, its weight and its trajectory, one had established the speed of light, worked at the ocean currents and the conditions of life, and soon it would be possible to solve the last riddle, magnetic force. The end of the road was in sight, the measuring of the world almost complete. The cosmos would be understood, all difficulties pertaining to man's beginnings, such as fear, war, and exploitation, would sink into the past, and Germany in particular and even more particularly the scientists gathered here tonight must give this their most urgent support. Science would bring about an era of the general good, and who could know if one day it might not even solve the problem of death. For a few moments Humboldt stood there, still. Then he bowed.

Since his return from Paris, whispered Daguerre under the cover of the applause, the baron hadn't been the same as he used to be. He was having difficulties concentrating. And he was inclined to repetition.

Gauss asked if it was true he'd come back because of lack of money.

Mostly because of an order, said Daguerre. The king had no longer been willing to tolerate his most famous subject making his home abroad. Humboldt had responded to all letters from the Court with evasions, but the last one contained such a clear warning that he could only resist it at the cost of making a complete break. And for that, Daguerre smiled, the old gentleman lacked sufficient funds. His long-awaited account of his journey had disappointed the public: hundreds of pages crammed with measurements, almost nothing personal, and for all intents and purposes no adventure. A tragic circumstance, it would curtail his fame. A renowned traveler was only renowned if he left good stories behind. The poor man had simply no idea how to write a book! Now he was sitting in Berlin, building an observatory, conceiving a thousand projects and getting on the nerves of the entire city council. The younger scientists made fun of him.

He didn't know how things were in Berlin. Gauss got to his feet. But in Göttingen he'd never met a young scientist who wasn't an ass.

Even the business about the highest mountain wasn't true, said Daguerre as he followed Gauss toward the exit. In the meantime it had been discovered that the Himalayas were far higher. A bad blow for the old man. For years he had refused to accept it. Beyond which he had never recovered from the collapse of his expedition to India.

On his way to the foyer Gauss jostled a woman, trod on a man's foot, and blew his nose twice so loudly that several officers gave him looks of contempt. He was quite unused to conducting himself in such a crowd of people. Intending to be helpful, Daguerre took his elbow, but Gauss let fly at him. Don't! He thought for a moment, then: a salt solution.

Oh yes, said Daguerre sympathetically.

Gauss told him not to gape at him like an idiot. One could fix silver iodide with a simple salt solution.

Daguerre stopped dead. Gauss pushed his way through the hubbub to Humboldt, whom he'd seen at the entrance to the foyer. Salt solution, Daguerre called out behind him. Why?

One didn't have to be a chemist for that, Gauss called back over his shoulder, all it took was a little understanding. He walked hesitantly into the foyer, applause broke out, and if Humboldt hadn't immediately seized him by the arm and pushed him forward, he would have fled. More than three hundred people had been awaiting him.

The next half hour was torture. One head after the other pushed itself in front of him, one hand after the other reached for his arm and passed it to the next hand, while Humboldt whispered a meaningless row of names into his ear. Gauss calculated that at home it would take him almost exactly a year and seven months to meet this many people. He wanted to go home. Half the men were in uniform, a third of them had mustaches. Only one seventh of the audience were women, only a quarter of these were under thirty, only two weren't ugly, and only one was someone he'd have liked to touch but seconds after she had curtseyed to him, she was already gone. A man with thirty-two bars of decorations held Gauss's hand negligently between three fingers, Gauss bowed mechanically, the crown prince nodded and moved on.

He didn't feel well, said Gauss, he had to go to bed.

He noticed his velvet cap was missing, someone had taken it from him, and he didn't know whether that was the usual thing or whether it had been stolen. A man clapped him on the shoulder as if they'd known each other for years, and possibly that might indeed be the case. While someone in uniform clicked his heels and someone else wearing spectacles and a frock coat swore that this was the greatest moment of his life, he felt tears coming up in his eyes. He thought of his mother.

Suddenly everything went still.

A thin old gentleman with waxy skin and unnaturally erect posture had come in. Taking tiny steps, apparently without moving his legs, he glided up to Humboldt. The two of them stretched out their arms, took each other by the shoulders, and bowed their heads a few centimeters, then each of them took one step back.

What a joy, said Humboldt.

Indeed, said the other.

The bystanders applauded. The two men waited until the applause had subsided, then turned to Gauss.

This, said Humboldt, was his beloved brother, the minister.

He knew, said Gauss. They had met in Weimar years ago.

Prussia's teacher, said Humboldt, who had given Germany its university and the world the true theory of language.

A world, said the minister, whose composition and natural organization had been unlocked by none other than his brother. His hand felt cold and lifeless, his eyes fixed like a doll's. Most of all, he was no longer a teacher, not for years. Only a private citizen and a poet.

Poet? Gauss was glad to be able to let go of his hand.

He dictated a sonnet every day to his secretary between seven and eight thirty in the evening. He'd been doing it for twelve years and would continue to do so until his death.

Gauss asked if they were good sonnets.

He certainly hoped so, said the minister. But now he must excuse himself.

Such a pity, said Humboldt.

Nonetheless, said the minister, a wonderful evening, a great pleasure.

The two of them stretched out their arms and repeated the ritual from before. The minister turned toward the door and went out with neat little steps.

An unexpected joy, said Humboldt again. Suddenly he looked depressed.

He wanted to go home, said Gauss.

A little longer, said Humboldt. This was Commander of the Gendarmerie Vogt, and science owed him a great deal. He was planning to issue all Berlin gendarmes with compasses. This would allow them to collect new data on magnetic field fluctuations across the capital. The Commandant of Gendarmerie was six feet six inches tall, with a walrus mustache and a terrifying handshake. And this, continued Humboldt, was Malzacher the zoologist, Rotter the chemist, and over here Weber the physicist from Halle and his wife.

Delighted, said Gauss, delighted. He was close to bursting into tears. All the same, the young woman had a small, well-shaped face, dark eyes, and a dress with a deep décolleté. He transferred his gaze to her in the hopes that it might cheer him up.

He was an experimental physicist, said Weber. Working on electrical forces. They tried to keep themselves hidden, but he wasn't giving them a chance.

That's the way he'd done it too, said Gauss, without taking his eyes off the pretty wife. With numbers. A long time ago.

He knew that, said Weber. He'd studied the *Disquisitiones* more closely than the Bible. Which admittedly he had never studied that closely at all.

The woman had delicate, very highly arched eyebrows. Her dress left her shoulders bare. Gauss wondered what it would be like to press his lips to those shoulders.

He dreamed, he heard Doctor Weber from Halle talking on, that a mind such as the professor's, in other words not a specialized mathematical mind but a universal one, one that solved problems wherever they presented themselves, would dedicate itself to an experimental exploration of the world. He had so many questions. It was his greatest wish to pose them to Professor Gauss.

He didn't have much time, said Gauss.

That might be, said Weber. But in all modesty, it was essential and he wasn't just nobody.

Gauss looked at him for the first time. A young man with a narrow face and pale eyes stood there in front of him.

He had to say it, explained Weber, smiling, for the sake of the project. He had studied the wave movements of electrical fields. His writings were widely read.

Gauss asked how old he was.

Twenty-four. Weber blushed.

You have a beautiful wife, said Gauss.

Weber said thank you. His wife bobbed a curtsey but didn't look embarrassed.

Your parents are proud of you?

He thought so, said Weber.

He was to come visit him next afternoon, said Gauss. He could have an hour, but then he'd have to take himself off.

That would do, said Weber.

Gauss nodded and went to the door. Humboldt called out that he must stay, the king was expected, but he couldn't do it any more, he was dead tired. The commander of gendarmerie with the big mustache stepped into his path, each of them went right and then left and then right again to try to get past the other, and it took several awkward moments before they succeeded. A warty man stood by the cloakroom surrounded by students, cursing in broad Swabian: natural scientist, know-it-all, no perspective, no grasp of dialectic, mindless, the stars too were mere matter! Gauss ran out onto the street.

He had pains in his stomach. Was it true that there were vehicles in big cities that one could simply stop and they would take one home? But there were none visible. It stank. At home he'd have been in bed long ago, and although he didn't like seeing Minna, didn't want to hear her voice, and nothing made him more nervous than her presence, he missed her out of pure habit. He rubbed his eyes. How had he grown so old? One didn't feel right any more, one didn't see right any more, and one thought at a snail's pace. Aging wasn't a tragedy. It was a farce.

He concentrated until he recalled every detail of the route Humboldt's coach had taken from Packhof number 4 to the Choral Hall. He didn't get every curve in the right order, but the direction seemed clear: obliquely to the left, northeast in fact. At home he would have settled it with one look upward, but in this sewer there were no stars to be seen. The light-extinguishing ether. If one lived here, that was the sort of idiocy that would occur to one!

At every step he glanced around. He was afraid of robbers, of dogs and filthy puddles. He worried that the city was so large that he would never find his way out again, that it was a labyrinth that would hold him fast and never let him go home. But no, one mustn't let mere nothings escalate! A city, a city was just houses, and in a hundred years the smallest of them would be bigger than these, and in three hundred years — he frowned, it was no simple task to calculate an exponential growth curve when one was nervous and unhappy and had stomach cramps, so in three hundred years there would be more people living in most towns than lived today in all the states of Germany combined. People like insects, housed in honeycombs, doing lowly jobs, siring children and dying. Of course the corpses would have to be burned, there would be no cemeteries large enough to cope. And all the excrement? He sneezed and wondered if he was now getting really ill.

When his host came home two hours later, he found Gauss in the big armchair, smoking a pipe, his feet up on a little Mexican stone table.

Where had he vanished to so abruptly, cried Humboldt, people had been looking for him, they had feared the worst, and there had been a magnificent buffet! The king had been disappointed.

He was sorry about the buffet, said Gauss.

It was no way to behave. Many people had journeyed here strictly on his account. One just couldn't do things like that!

He liked that Weber, said Gauss. But light-extinguishing ether? Absolute rubbish.

Humboldt crossed his arms.

Occam's razor, said Gauss. The number of hypotheses required to arrive at an explanation should be as small as possible. Moreover space was certainly empty, but it was curved. The stars were wandering through a very eerie vault.

That again, said Humboldt. Astral geometry. He had to say he was astonished that a man like Gauss would champion such a line of thought.

Not what he was doing, said Gauss. He had decided early on never to publish anything on the subject. He had had no desire to lay himself open to mockery. Too many people held their own assumptions to be the fundamental laws of the universe. He blew two little clouds of smoke up toward the ceiling. What an evening! He almost had got lost on the way home and in order to be let in by the lazy staff, he'd had to wake the whole household. There couldn't be filthier streets anywhere.

Being possibly more traveled, he could correct that, said Humboldt sharply. And he assured him there were filthier ones. And it was a major mistake just to walk off when so many people had come together who could help set projects in motion.

Projects, snorted Gauss. Plans, intrigues. A whole palaver with ten princes and a hundred members of the Academy before you were even allowed to put up a barometer somewhere. It wasn't science.

Oh, cried Humboldt, so what was science, then?

Gauss pulled on his pipe. A man alone at his desk. A sheet of paper in front of him, at most a telescope as well, and a clear sky outside the window. If such a man didn't give up before he reached an understanding, that, perhaps, was science.

And if this man went on journeys?

Gauss gave a slight shrug. Whatever was hiding way out there in holes or volcanoes or mines was accidental, unimportant. That wasn't how the world would become clearer.

This man at his desk, said Humboldt, would naturally need a nurturing wife to warm his feet and cook his food, along with numerous children to clean his instruments and parents who tended him like a baby. And a solid house with a good roof against the rain. And a cap so that he would never get earache.

Gauss asked what he meant by that.

He was speaking in general.

In that case: yes, he'd need all that and more. How else would a man survive?

The servant, in his nightshirt already, came in.

Humboldt asked what kind of manners these were, couldn't he even knock?

The servant gave him a piece of paper. It had just been handed in, by a street urchin. It seemed to be important.

Uninteresting, said Humboldt. He didn't accept letters at night from who-knew-who. It was like something out of a play by Kotzebue! Reluctantly he unfolded the paper and read it. Curious, he said. A poem. Terribly badly rhymed. Something about trees, wind, and the sea. There was also a raven and a medieval king. Then it stopped. Obviously no one could find a rhyme for *silver*.

The servant asked him to turn the piece of paper over.

Humboldt did so, and read. Dear God, he said quietly.

Gauss sat up.

Apparently young Mr. Eugen had got himself into difficulties. He had smuggled this out of the police prison.

Gauss stared at the ceiling, motionless.

This was really rather unpleasant, said Humboldt. He was, after all, a state official.

Gauss nodded.

And nor could he help. Things would take their course. Besides one could rely on Prussian justice, there would be no miscarriage. If someone had done nothing, there was nothing to fear.

Gauss looked at his pipe.

It was shaming, said Humboldt, most vexatious. Nonetheless it involved his guest.

There had never been a thing you could do with the boy, said Gauss. He pushed the pipe stem between his teeth.

They were silent for a while. Humboldt stepped over to the window and stared down into the dark courtyard.

So what could one do?

Yes, said Gauss.

It had been a long day, said Humboldt. They were both tired.

And neither of them so young any more, said Gauss.

Humboldt went to the door and said good night.

He would finish his pipe, said Gauss.

243

Humboldt picked up the candelabrum and closed the door behind him.

Gauss folded his hands behind his head. The only light came from the glow of his pipe. Down on the street a vehicle rolled by with a tinny noise. Gauss took his pipe out of his mouth and twisted it between his fingers. He pursed his lips and cocked his head. Steps were coming closer, then the door flew open.

It wasn't acceptable, cried Humboldt, he would not tolerate it!

So, said Gauss.

But there wasn't much time. Tonight Eugen would still be in the custody of the gendarmes. First thing tomorrow the secret police would take over, then it would be impossible to stop anything. If they wanted to get him out, it had to be now.

Gauss asked if he knew how late it was.

Humboldt stared at him.

He hadn't been up and about at this hour for years. If he thought about it properly, he hadn't ever done it at all.

Humboldt, disbelieving, set down the candelabrum.

So all right. Gauss sniffed, laid down his pipe, and got to his feet. It was unquestionably going to make him sicker.

He looked perfectly well to him, said Humboldt.

That was quite enough, cried Gauss. Things were bad as it was. He didn't have to let himself be insulted!

Spirits

Commander of Gendarmerie Vogt had gone out. His wife, wrapped in a woolen housecoat, face and hair still rumpled with sleep, told them he had come home briefly after the reception at the Choral Hall, and then was called away, apparently there had been some arrests. He had come back again shortly before midnight, had changed into civilian clothes, and then gone off again. It happened like that once a week. No, she didn't know where.

Then there was nothing to be done, said Humboldt. He bowed and made to leave.

He thought, said Gauss.

The two of them looked at him questioningly.

He thought that there was something they could do. Humboldt had never been married so he didn't know how things went. A wife whose husband was out once a week at night knew very well where he was hiding himself, and if he didn't give it away himself, she found out anyway. And now she could do a great favor for two old gentlemen.

She really couldn't say a thing, murmured Frau Vogt.

Gauss took a step closer, laid his hand on her arm, and asked why she was making it so hard for them. Did he and his friend look like informers, like the kind of people who couldn't keep a secret? He lowered his head and smiled at her. It was really important.

But nobody must know it came from her.

Of course not, said Gauss.

It wasn't anything forbidden. And it had only started since the death of the grandmother. There were suspicions that there was hidden money somewhere, but nobody knew where. So they were trying everything they could.

See, same old thing, said Gauss as they were going down the stairs. Women could never keep their mouths shut. If the wife knew, everyone would know. Could they please stop for a moment at the police station? He wanted to check on the good-for-nothing.

Impossible, said Humboldt. He couldn't allow himself to be seen there.

The leading Republican in Europe couldn't go into a police jail?

The leading Republican in particular, said Humboldt. His position was more fragile than might be apparent at first glance. Not even fame was always a protection. Navigating the Orinoco had been easier than navigating this city. He lowered his voice. In the police jail the gendarmerie divided prisoners strictly by rank; their particulars would only be taken down by the secret police the following morning. If they could succeed in persuading Vogt to send the young man home at once, no trace of him would be left in the records.

The boy was hopeless, said Gauss. He liked that Weber person much better.

One couldn't choose these things, said Humboldt.

Apparently not, said Gauss, and said nothing more until the coach came to a halt.

They went through a dirty courtyard and up some stairs. Twice they had to pause until Gauss could catch his breath again. They reached the third floor, and Humboldt knocked on the apartment door. A pale man with an elaborately combed, pointed beard opened up. He was wearing a gold-embroidered shirt, velvet trousers, and worn bedroom slippers.

Lorenzi, he said. It took them several seconds to grasp that he had introduced himself.

Humboldt asked if the commander of gendarmerie were there.

He was there, said Herr Lorenzi in stumbling German, along with a number of other people. But anyone who wanted to come in must join the circle.

All right, said Gauss.

The circle must not be broken, said Lorenzi, must not be torn apart in this world or the next. In other words, it would cost money.

Gauss shook his head but Humboldt stuck some gold coins in Lorenzi's hand and the latter stepped aside with a bow.

The hall was laid with worn-out carpets. Through a half-open door they could hear a woman's voice, wailing. They went in.

The room was lit by a single candle. People were sitting around a large table. The wailing was coming from a girl of about seventeen, wearing a white nightdress. Her face was covered in sweat and her hair clung to her forehead. To her left, eyes closed, sat Commander of Gendarmerie Vogt. Next to him, a man with a bald head, three older ladies, a woman in black, and several gentlemen in dark suits. The girl rolled her head and groaned. Humboldt wanted to go out again, but Gauss stopped him. Lorenzi pushed up two chairs. Hesitantly they sat down at the table.

And now, said Lorenzi, they must all hold each other's hands.

Not on his life, said Humboldt.

It wasn't so bad, said Gauss, and seized Lorenzi's hand. If they got thrown out, it wouldn't help either.

No, said Humboldt.

Then it wouldn't work, said Lorenzi.

Gauss sighed and reached for Humboldt's left hand, just as a woman of about sixty who looked like a statue that had been left out in the rain reached for his right. Humboldt went rigid.

The girl tossed her head back and screamed. Her nightdress slipped down as she twisted violently. Gauss looked at her with raised eyebrows. Her body leapt into the air as if she wanted to jump up, but the two men to either side of her held her fast; she bared her teeth, her eyes rolled, she rocked from side to side and whimpered. She had seen King Solomon, she panted, but he didn't want to come so now she was summoning someone else.

He wasn't going to be able to stand this, said Humboldt.

248

It was actually quite fun, said Gauss. And the little one wasn't bad at all.

She screamed loudly, a tremor threw her body backwards; if the men hadn't been holding her, she and her chair would have tipped over. Then she became calmer again, laid her head to one side, and stared at the tabletop. Someone was here, she said. He wanted his uncle to know that everything was forgiven. A son was waiting for his mother. And further off she could see Napoleon, the devil in human form, burning in hell. He was uttering horrible blasphemies and wouldn't repent. She turned her head to listen. Her nightdress was hanging open down beyond her breast. Her skin glistened damply. She could see someone else's brother, she said, he was saying his death was natural and wholly in order, there was no need to keep making enquiries. And someone else's mother. The mother was very disappointed. Her son's work would turn out to be insignificant, she knew now that he'd only been waiting for her to die so that he could run off like a vagabond, and in the cave that time he'd behaved as if he didn't see her. Then there was a child there, who was letting his parents know he was doing quite well in the circumstances, the hall was large, they could fly all the time, and if you were careful, no pain was inflicted on you. And an old lady was saying that she hadn't hidden any money and couldn't help. The girl groaned, everyone leaned forward, but nothing more came out. She made a strangled noise, then raised her head, gently freed her hands from the grip of the men, pulled up and straightened her nightdress, and smiled at no one in particular in a confused sort of way.

Good, said Gauss.

Vogt, startled, looked at him across the table. He had only just noticed them.

A word, please, said Humboldt. He was white, and his face looked like a mask.

Fascinating, said the woman in black.

A unique moment of communication between the worlds, said Lorenzi. Everyone looked at him reproachfully, he had spoken without an Italian accent; hastily he said it again the proper way. The girl glanced around, embarrassed. Gauss was watching her alertly.

Vogt asked if they'd followed him.

After a fashion, said Humboldt. He had a request. A conversation à deux. He made a sign to Gauss to stay where he was and went out into the hall with Vogt. He was here because of his grandmother, Vogt whispered. Nobody knew where the money was. His situation wasn't easy. A gentleman must pay his debts, come what may. And that's why he was trying everything.

Humboldt cleared his throat, and closed his eyes for a moment or two as if to pull himself together. A young man, he said, the son of the astronomer over there, had got himself arrested at some foolish gathering. There was still time to simply send him home again.

Vogt stroked his mustache.

One would be doing one's country a service. Prussia was very deeply committed to working with this man. It was in the highest interests of state.

In the highest interests of state, Vogt echoed.

In other countries, said Humboldt, decorations were given for this kind of thing.

Vogt leaned against the wall. What was being proposed was no mere trifle. A most suspicious secret assembly. At first it had been thought that the appalling writer of *German Gymnastics* had spoken in person. Now, praise be to God, it appeared that the speaker had been merely one of his many imitators who went around the country using his name. But an express courier was on his way to Freiberg in any case, just to be certain.

Ah, the plague of mistaken identities, said Humboldt. Two of his colleagues, Daguerre and Niepce, were working on an invention which would help in this situation. Authorities would then have official pictures of people, and nobody would be able to pass themselves off as someone famous any more. He knew the problem well, just recently some man in the Tyrol had lived for months on the public funds, because he had claimed to be Humboldt and to know how to find gold.

In any case, said Vogt, the situation was serious. He wasn't saying that nothing could be done. He looked at Humboldt expectantly. But it wouldn't be easy.

All he had to do was go to the police jail and send the young man home, said Humboldt. The name hadn't even been registered. Nobody would know.

But there was a risk, said Vogt.

But a small one.

Small or not, between civilized people there were ways of recognizing these things.

Humboldt assured him of his gratitude.

Which could express itself in more than one way.

Humboldt promised that he would have a friend in him. And he would be ready to grant any favor.

Favor. Vogt sighed. There were favors and favors.

Humboldt asked what he meant.

Vogt groaned. They looked at each other in embarrassment.

God almighty, said Gauss's voice beside them. Did he really not understand? The fellow wanted a bribe. Poor pathetic little fellow. Poor little shit-eater.

He must protest, shrilled Vogt. He didn't have to listen to such things!

Humboldt made frantic hand signals at Gauss. Everyone came out of the salon full of curiosity: the bald-headed man and the woman in black whispered to each other while the girl in the nightdress looked at them over her shoulder.

Yes he damn well did, said Gauss. Even a piece of vomit like him, a bastard mongrel, a greedy dwarf turd, should be able to bear up under the truth.

That was quite enough, shrieked Vogt.

Nothing like enough, said Gauss.

He would dispatch his seconds in the morning.

For God's sake, cried Humboldt, it was all a misunderstanding.

He would throw them out, said Gauss. They would be bound to be a pair of ne'er-do-wells if they were willing to be ordered around by a dung beetle like him.

They could expect to learn the size of his foot, in the ass and elsewhere!

In a tight voice Vogt enquired if this was meant to indicate that the gentleman was refusing him satisfaction.

Of course it did. Was he going to allow himself to be shot dead by a stink toad?

Vogt opened and closed his mouth, balled his fists, and stared at the ceiling. His chin quivered. If he had understood correctly, the son of the professor was in some difficulties. The professor should not expect to see his son again any time soon. He stumbled to the coat stand, seized his coat and the nearest hat, and ran out.

But that was his hat, called the bald-headed man, running after him.

Well, that didn't work, said Gauss eventually into the general silence. He threw another long glance at the medium, then pushed his hands into his pockets and left the apartment.

A frightful mistake, said Humboldt, as he caught up with him on the stairs. The man hadn't wanted any money!

Ha, said Gauss.

A high official of the Prussian state could not be bribed. Such a thing had never happened.

Ha!

He would lay his hand in the fire!

Gauss laughed.

They stepped into the open air and discovered that their coach had left.

Well then, on foot, said Humboldt. It wasn't that far, and as for him, he'd mastered much greater distances in his time.

Please not again, said Gauss. He couldn't listen to it any more.

The two of them looked at each other, furious, then set off.

It was age, said Humboldt after a bit. Once upon a time he'd been able to convince anyone. Overcome every obstacle, get any passport he wanted. No one had ever resisted him.

Gauss didn't answer. They walked along in silence.

Well all right, said Gauss finally. He admitted it. It hadn't been clever of him. But he'd made him so angry!

A medium like her should be put out of business, said Humboldt. It was no way to approach the dead. Indecent, was what it was — brazen and vulgar. He had grown up with spirits, and he knew how one behaved toward them.

These lanterns, said Gauss. Soon they would be lit by gas, and night would be banished. They were both growing old in a second-class era. What would happen to Eugen now?

Expelled from university. Prison, probably. In certain circumstances they could arrange for him to be exiled.

Gauss said nothing.

Sometimes one had to accept, said Humboldt, that one couldn't help people. It had taken him years to come to terms with the fact that he could do nothing for Bonpland. He couldn't grieve about it day after day.

The only thing was that he was going to have to tell Minna. She was idiotically fond of the boy.

If something was going to fail, said Humboldt, you just had to let it fail, you couldn't stop it. It didn't sound nice, but this was just the harder side, the brutal side one might say, of success in life.

His life was over, said Gauss. He had a home that meant nothing to him, a daughter nobody wanted, and a son who'd landed in a disaster. And his mother wasn't long for this world. For the last fifteen years he'd been measuring hills. He stood still and looked up into the night sky. All in all, he couldn't explain why he felt so lighthearted.

He couldn't either, said Humboldt. But he felt the same way.

Perhaps this thing and that were still possible. Magnetism. The geometry of space. His head wasn't what it once was, but then again it wasn't useless.

He had never been to Asia, said Humboldt. That was not an appropriate state of affairs. He found himself wondering if it was not in fact a mistake to rule out the invitation to Russia.

Naturally he would need new collaborators. He couldn't do it on his own any more. His eldest son was in the army, the youngest was still too young, and Eugen was out of the picture. But he'd taken to the Weber fellow. And he had a pretty wife! There was a vacant post of professor of physics at Göttingen.

It wouldn't be easy, said Humboldt. The regime would want to control him every step of the way. But if anyone thought he was weak or submissive, they'd made a mistake. They'd kept him away from India. But he would go to Russia.

Experimental physics, said Gauss. Something new. He'd have to think about it.

With any luck, said Humboldt, he could even get as far as China.

The Steppes

What, ladies and gentlemen, is death? Fundamentally it is not extinction and those seconds when life ends, but the slow decline that precedes it, that creeping debility that extends over years: the time in which a person is still there and yet not there, in which he can still imagine that although his prime is long since past, it lingers yet. So circumspectly, ladies and gentlemen, has nature organized our death!

When the applause ended, Humboldt had already left the podium. A coach was waiting outside the Choral Hall to take him to his sister-in-law, who was lying on her sickbed. She was gently sinking away, without pain, between sleep and semiconsciousness. She opened her eyes one last time, looked first at Humboldt, then, a little frightened, at her husband, as if she had difficulty distinguishing between them. Seconds later she was gone. Afterwards the brothers sat together facing each other; Humboldt held his elder brother's hand, because he knew the situation required it, but for a time they totally forgot to sit up straight and say classical things.

Did he remember the evening, his elder brother asked finally, when they read the story of Aguirre and he decided to go to the Orinoco? It was a date the world would remember!

Of course he remembered, said Humboldt. But he no longer believed the future world would care, he also had doubts about the significance of the journey upriver itself. The channel didn't produce any benefit for the continent, it was as abandoned and mosquito-ridden as ever, Bonpland had been right. At least he had spent his life without being bored.

Boredom had never troubled him, said the elder brother. He had just not wanted to be alone.

He had always been alone, said Humboldt, but it was boredom that had terrified him to death.

He had found it very hard, said the elder brother, that he had never been made chancellor of Germany, but Hardenberg had prevented it, though it had always been his destiny.

Nobody, said Humboldt, had a destiny. One simply decided to feign one until one came to believe in it oneself. But so many things didn't fit in with it, one had to really force oneself.

The elder brother leaned back and gave him a long look. Still boys?

You knew?

Always.

Neither of them spoke for a long while, then Humboldt rose and they embraced as formally as ever.

Will we see each other again?

Certainly. In the flesh or in the light.

He was awaited at the Academy by his two traveling companions, Ehrenberg the zoologist and the mineralogist Rose. Ehrenberg was short, fat, and had a pointed beard. Rose was more than six foot six and seemed to have perpetually damp hair. Both wore thick glasses. The court had allotted them to Humboldt as his assistants. Together they checked over all the equipment: the cyanometer, the telescope, and the Leyden jar from his trip to the tropics, an English clock that ran more accurately than the old French one, and for measuring magnetism, a better dipping compass needle made by Gamberg himself, and also an iron-free tent. Then Humboldt had himself taken to Charlottenburg Palace.

He saluted this journey into the empire of his son-in-law, said Friedrich Wilhelm slowly. So he was elevating Chamberlain Humboldt to the position of True Private Adviser, who from now on was to be addressed as Excellence.

Humboldt was so moved that he had to turn away.

What is it, Alexander?

It was only, said Humboldt hastily, because of the death of his sister-in-law.

He knew Russia, said the king, and he also knew Humboldt's reputation. He wished for there to be no problems! It was not necessary to weep tears over every unhappy peasant.

He had given his assurances to the tsar, said Humboldt in a tone that sounded as if he'd learned the words by heart. He would occupy himself with inanimate nature; he would not be studying the relations of the lower classes. It was a sentence he had already written twice to the tsar and three times to high officials of the Prussian Court.

At home there were two letters. One from the elder brother, thanking him for the visit and his support. Whether we see each other again or not, now once more, it is just we two, as it always was fundamentally. We were inculcated early with the lesson that life requires an audience. We both believed that the whole world was ours. Little by little the circles became smaller, and we were forced to realize that the actual goal of all our efforts was not the cosmos but merely each other. Because of you I wanted to become a minister, because of me you had to conquer the highest mountain and the deepest caverns, for you I founded the greatest university, for me you discovered South America, and only fools who fail to understand the significance of a single life in double form would describe this as a rivalry: because there was you, I had to become the teacher of my country, because there was me, you had to become the scientist who explored an entire continent; nothing else would have been appropriate. And we always had the most acute sense of what was appropriate. I beg you not to allow this letter to be found sometime in the future with the rest of our correspondence, even if, as you yourself told me, you no longer hold any brief for the future.

The other letter was from Gauss. He too sent his good wishes along with several formulae for magnetic measurements of which Humboldt understood not one line. Besides this, he recommended that Humboldt learn Russian along the way. He himself had recently begun to do the same, not least as the result of a long-standing promise. Should Humboldt encounter a certain Pushkin, would he please not forget to assure him of his great admiration.

The servant came in and announced that everything was ready, the horses had been fed, the instruments loaded, they would be set to leave at dawn.

In point of fact Russian really did help Gauss survive the aggravation at home, Minna's endless wailing and reproaches, his daughter's sad face, and all the questions about Eugen. Nina had given him the Russian dictionary as a parting present: she had gone to her sister in East Prussia, leaving Göttingen forever. For a moment he had wondered if she, and not Johanna, had been the woman of his life.

He had softened. Recently he had even succeeded in looking at Minna without distaste. There was something in her narrow, elderly, perpetually complaining face that he would miss if she were no longer there.

Weber was writing to him frequently now. It did seem likely that he would soon be coming to Göttingen. The professorship was opening up and Gauss's word carried weight. Such a pity, he said to his daughter, that you're so ugly and he already has a wife!

On the return journey from Berlin, when the swaying of the coach had made him more ill than ever in his life before, he had tried to help himself by thinking through the shuddering, shaking, and rolling to their fundamentals. Slowly but surely he managed to separate out all the parts of the whole combination. It really didn't help much, but in the process he had understood the principle of the smallest possible force: every movement corresponded with that of the system as a whole for as long as it could. The moment he had reached Göttingen in the early hours of the morning, he had sent Weber the notes he'd made, and Weber had returned them with clever comments. The paper would be published in a few months. So now he'd become a physicist.

In the afternoons he took long walks through the woods. Over time he'd ceased to get lost, he knew this area better than anyone, after all he'd fixed every detail of it on the map. Sometimes it was as if he hadn't just measured the region, but invented it, as if it had only achieved its reality through him. Where once there had been nothing but trees, peat bogs, stones, and grassy mounds, there was now a net of grades, angles, and numbers. Nothing someone had ever measured was now or ever could be the same as before. Gauss wondered if Humboldt would understand that. It began to rain, and he took shelter under a tree. The grass shivered, it smelled of fresh earth, and there was nowhere else he could ever want to be but here.

Humboldt's baggage train was not making much progress. His departure had coincided with the time of the spring thaw; a failure in planning of a kind he had never committed before. The coaches sank into the mud or kept sliding off the water-logged roads; again and again they had to halt and wait. The column was too long, there were too many of them. They were already late by the time they reached Königsberg.

Professor Bessel greeted Humboldt with a rhetorical deluge, led them through the new observatory, and had his guests shown the greatest collection of amber in the country.

Humboldt asked him if he hadn't once worked with Professor Gauss.

The high point of his life, said Bessel, if not exactly easy. The moment in Bremen when the Prince of Mathematics had recommended that he give up science and become a cook or a blacksmith, if neither of these was too much of a challenge, was one from which he'd taken a long time to recover. Nonetheless he had been lucky; his friend Bartels in Petersburg had had an even harder time with him. In the face of such superiority, the only thing that helped was sympathy.

On the next stage of the journey, to Tilsit, the roads were covered in ice, and several times the wagons broke down. At the Russian border they found a troop of Cossacks under orders to accompany them.

That really wasn't necessary, said Humboldt.

He must trust him, said the commander, it was necessary.

He had spent years in the wilderness without protective escort!

This wasn't the wilderness, said the commander. This was Russia.

Outside Dorpat there were a dozen journalists waiting, along with the entire Faculty of Sciences. The first thing they wanted to do was show them the mineralogical and botanical collections.

Gladly, said Humboldt, though in fact he was here not for the museums but for Nature.

Let him take care of that in the meantime, offered Rose, eager to be useful, that shouldn't hold them up, that was precisely why he'd come!

While Rose was measuring the hills around the town, the mayor, the dean of the university, and two officers led Humboldt through an unbelievably long suite of poorly ventilated rooms full of samples of amber. One of the stones held a spider of a kind Humboldt had never seen before, and in another there was an extraordinary winged scorpion, which deserved to be called a fabulous creature. Humboldt held the stone up close to his eyes and blinked, but it did no good, he didn't see well any more. He must have a drawing of it made!

Of course, said Ehrenberg, who all of a sudden was standing right behind him, as he took the stone from his hand and bore it away. Humboldt wanted to call him back, but then he let it go. It would have looked strange in front of all these people. He didn't get the drawing and he never saw the stone again. When he asked Ehrenberg about it later, he couldn't remember anything.

They left Dorpat in the direction of the capital. An imperial courier rode ahead, two officers had attached themselves to them along with three professors and a geologist from the Petersburg Academy, one Volodin, who Humboldt kept forgetting was there, so that he gave a start every time Volodin chimed in with some comment in his light, quiet voice. It was as if something in this pale figure resisted being fixed into memory, or as if it commanded to perfection the art of rendering itself invisible. At the river Narva they had to wait two days for the ice to yield. In the meantime their numbers had swollen to the point where they needed the large ferry to cross, and it could only do that when the river was completely clear. So they were late in reaching St. Petersburg.

The Prussian ambassador accompanied Humboldt to his audience. The tsar held his hand for a long time, assured him that his visit was an honor for Russia, and asked about Humboldt's elder brother, whom he remembered clearly from the Congress of Vienna.

Did he remember him fondly?

Well, said the tsar, to be frank he had always found him rather intimidating.

Every European envoy gave a reception for Humboldt. He dined several times with the imperial family. The finance minister, Count Cancrin, doubled the promised travel funds.

He was grateful, said Humboldt, although he did think with longing of the days when he had financed his travels on his own.

No reason for longing, said Cancrin, he had every freedom and this, he pushed a piece of paper at Humboldt, was the route that would be permitted. He would be escorted along the way, he was expected at every stopping point, and all provincial garrisons were under orders to provide for his safety.

He wasn't sure, said Humboldt. He wanted to move about freely. A scientist must be able to improvise.

265

Only if he'd failed to plan properly, Cancrin reproached him with a smile. And this plan, he could promise him, was outstanding.

Before they went on to Moscow, Humboldt got letters again: two from his elder brother, whom loneliness was rendering talkative. A long letter from Bessel. And a card from Gauss from the depths of his experiments in magnetism. He was taking the thing seriously now, he had had a custom-designed windowless hut built, with an airtight door, and nails of unmagnetizable copper.

At first the town councilors had thought he'd gone mad. But Gauss had cursed them at such length, threatening and wailing and dangling so many totally invented advantages for trade and the economy and the town's fame before their eyes that they finally agreed and had put up the hut next to the observatory. Now he was spending the majority of his days in front of a long hanging iron needle in a galvanometer. Its movement was so weak as to be invisible to the naked eye; one had to direct a telescope at a mirror set up over the needle to see the minuscule oscillations of the movable scale. Humboldt's supposition was correct: the earth's field fluctuated, its strength altered periodically. But Gauss was measuring in shorter intervals than he had, he was measuring more accurately, and naturally he measured better; it amused him that it had eluded Humboldt that one had to take into account the stretching of the thread from which the needle was suspended.

Gauss observed the movement by the light of an oil lamp for hour after hour. No sound penetrated to him.

Just as the balloon flight with Pilâtre long ago had shown him what space was, at some point now he would understand the restlessness in the heart of Nature. One didn't need to clamber up mountains or torment oneself in the jungle. Whoever observed the needle was looking into the interior of the world. Sometimes his thoughts turned to his family. He missed Eugen, and Minna hadn't been well since the boy was not there. His youngest would soon finish school. He wasn't particularly intelligent either, and certainly wouldn't become a student. One had to accept it, one must not overestimate people. At least he was getting on better and better with Weber, and just recently a Russian mathematician had sent him a paper in which the supposition was laid out that Euclid's geometry was not the true geometry, and parallel lines did meet. Since he had written back to say that none of these ideas was new to him, he was considered in Russia to be a pretender.

At the thought that others would make public things he had known for so long, he felt an unaccustomed stab of pain. So he had had to reach this age before he learned what ambition was. Now and again, as he stared at the needle without daring to breathe, so as not to disturb its silent dance, he saw himself as a magus from the dark ages, like an alchemist in an engraving. But why not? The *Scientia Nova* had come out of magic, and some whiff of that would always remain.

Carefully he unfolded the map of Russia. What needed to be done was to distribute huts like this one all across the wastes of Siberia, to be inhabited by

267

reliable men who understood how to pay attention to instruments, spend hour after hour in front of telescopes, and lead a silent, watchful existence. Humboldt was good at organizing things, probably he could handle this too, Gauss thought. As he finished the list of the designated statistics, his youngest son tore open the door and brought him a letter. Wind shot in, papers flew through the air, the needle erupted in panicked movements, and Gauss boxed the child's ears twice with a force he would not forget in a hurry. Only after a half hour of sitting still and waiting had the compass settled sufficiently for Gauss to dare make a movement and open the letter. Plans would have to be changed, wrote Humboldt, he couldn't do anything he wished, a route had been prescribed, and he didn't think it sensible to deviate from it, he could measure along it but nowhere else, and he would try to adjust the calculations accordingly. Gauss laid aside the letter, smiling sadly. For the first time he felt sorry for Humboldt.

In Moscow everything came to a halt. It was quite impossible, said the mayor, that his honored guest should set out again right away. Whether it was a suitable time of year or not was neither here nor there, society awaited him, he simply could not deny Moscow what he had granted to St. Petersburg. So here, too, every evening, while Rose and Ehrenberg collected rock samples in the vicinity, Humboldt had to attend a dinner; toasts were offered, men in evening dress waved their glasses and cried Vivat, and trumpeters blew their instruments out of tune, and someone was always enquiring sympathetically if Humboldt didn't feel well. Of course he did, he replied and watched the setting sun, it was just that he'd never been fond of music and did it really have to be so loud?

It took weeks before he was given permission to set out for the Urals. Even more escorts had attached themselves, and it took an entire day for all the coaches to be made ready for the journey.

It was beyond belief, said Humboldt to Ehrenberg, he would not tolerate it, this was no expedition any longer!

One couldn't always do as one wished, was Rose's contribution.

And besides, asked Ehrenberg, what was the drawback? They were all clever, honorable people, they could relieve him of any work that was perhaps too much for him. Humboldt flushed with anger. But before he could say anything, the coaches started moving and his answer was submerged in the squeaking of wheels and the clattering of hooves.

At Nizhni Novgorod he established the breadth of the Volga with his sextant. For half an hour he stared through the eyepiece, swiveled the alidade, and murmured calculations. The escort watched respectfully. It was, said Volodin to Rose, as if they were experiencing a journey in time, as if they'd been transported into a history book, it was sublime. It made him want to cry!

Finally Humboldt announced that the river was five thousand two hundred and forty point seven feet wide.

But of course it was, said Rose soothingly.

Two hundred and forty point nine, to be exact, said Ehrenberg. But he had to admit it was a pretty good result given how old the method was.

In the city Humboldt was given salt, bread, and a golden key, was named an honorary citizen, had to listen to the offerings of a children's choir and participate in fourteen official and twenty-one unofficial private receptions before they were allowed onto a guard boat to sail up the Volga. At Kazan he insisted on carrying out magnetic measurements. He had the iron-free tent set up on open land, asked for quiet, crawled into it, and attached the compass to the prespecified suspension system. It took him longer than usual, because his hands were trembling, and the wind had started to make his eyes water. The needle swung hesitantly, steadied itself, held still for several minutes, then began to swing again. Humboldt thought of Gauss, a sixth of the earth's circumference away, who was doing the same thing. The poor man had never seen anything of the world. Humboldt gave a melancholy smile, suddenly he was feeling sorry for Gauss. Rose tapped on the surface of the tent from outside and asked if possibly things might go a little faster.

As they continued on their way they passed a column of convict women, escorted by mounted lancers. Humboldt wanted to halt and talk to them.

Out of the question, said Rose.

Completely unthinkable, Ehrenberg agreed. He banged on the roof and the coach moved off; within minutes their cloud of dust had swallowed up the column.

In Perm, as was now the routine, Ehrenberg and Rose set themselves to gathering rocks while Humboldt dined with the governor. The governor had four brothers, eight sons, five daughters, twenty-seven grandchildren, and nine great-grandchildren, along with an indeterminate number of cousins. They were all there and wanted to hear stories about the land across the sea. He didn't know anything, said Humboldt, he could barely remember, he would really like to go to bed.

Next morning he gave instructions for the collection to be divided: they needed two of every sample, which had to be transported separately.

But they'd been working with divided collections for years, said Rose.

All along, said Ehrenberg.

No sensible scientist did it any other way, said Rose. Everyone was familiar with Humboldt's writings.

They reached Ekaterinburg. The merchant with whom Humboldt was provided lodging had a beard, like everyone here, and wore a long tunic and a sash. When Humboldt returned home late in the evening from the mayor's reception, his host wanted to drink with him. Humboldt declined, the man began to sob like a child, smote his breast, and cried in terrible French that he was wretched, wretched, wretched, and he wanted to die.

Well all right, said Humboldt unhappily, but just one glass!

The vodka made Humboldt so ill that he had to spend two days in bed. For reasons no one could fathom, the administration set a Cossack guard in front of the house, and two officers were not to be deterred from spending the nights snoring in one corner of his room.

When he was able to get up again, Ehrenberg, Rose, and Volodin took him to an open goldmine. The captain of the mine, named Ossipov, was occupied with the question of what could be done against seepage. He took Humboldt into a flooded tunnel: the water was hip-deep and it stank of mold. Humboldt looked down mistrustfully at his sodden trouser legs.

It needed to be better pumped!

They didn't have enough equipment, said Ossipov worriedly.

Then, said Humboldt, they just needed more.

Ossipov asked how it was supposed to be paid for.

Fewer floods, said Humboldt shortly, and they could produce more.

Ossipov looked at him enquiringly.

That way the pumps paid for themselves, didn't they?

Ossipov thought, then seized Humboldt and hugged him to his chest.

On the next stage of the journey, Humboldt caught a fever. He had pains in his neck and his nose ran ceaselessly. A cold, he said, and wrapped himself tighter in his blanket. Could the coachman not go more slowly, he wasn't seeing anything of the pine forests!

Alas, said Rose, it wasn't something one could ask of Russian coachmen, that was how they had learned to drive, they didn't know any other way.

They didn't stop until they reached the famous Magnet Mountain. In the middle of the plain of Visokaya Gora a massive yellowish excrescence reared up into the sky, all compasses lost their bearings, and Humboldt started to climb. It was harder going than in earlier days, but certainly his cold was at fault; several times he had to let himself be supported by Ehrenberg, and when he wanted to bend down to get a rock, his back hurt so much that he asked Rose to take over the collecting. This was unnecessary since the director of the local ironworks was already waiting at the summit to present him with a little chest filled with carefully sorted earth samples. Humboldt thanked him hoarsely. The wind tore angrily at his woolen wrap.

So, said Rose, back down again?

In the ironworks a little boy was brought forward. His name was Pavel, said the mine director, he was fourteen and very stupid. But he'd found this stone. The child opened a dirty hand.

Clearly a diamond, said Humboldt after a thorough inspection.

Enormous jubilation broke out, the mine superintendents clapped one another on the shoulders, workmen danced, the male choir started up again, several of the miners gave Pavel friendly but very firm smacks on the ear.

Not bad, said Volodin. Only a few weeks in the country and he'd already found Russia's first diamond, one could feel the hand of the master.

He hadn't found it, said Humboldt.

If he might give him a word of advice, said Rose, it would be better not to repeat that sentence.

There was a superficial truth, and then there was a deeper one, said Ehrenberg, Germans in particular understood this.

Was it too much to ask, said Rose, to give the people what they wanted, just for one moment?

A few days later they were overtaken by a totally exhausted horseman bringing a letter of thanks from the tsar.

Humboldt's cold didn't clear up. They drove through the taiga in clouds of insects. The sky was extremely high and it seemed that the sun no longer went down any more, so night became a vague memory. The distance, with its grassy marshes, low trees, and snaking streams, dissolved in a white haze. Sometimes, when Humboldt jerked awake in shock after a few moments of sleep and realized that the needle of the chronometer had jumped yet another hour, the sky with its small puffs of clouds and the relentlessly burning sun seemed divided into segments and interlaced with cracks that receded along with his field of vision whenever he turned his head.

A watchful Ehrenberg asked if another blanket might be desired.

He had never used two blankets, said Humboldt. But Ehrenberg, unmoved, held out the blanket and weakness overcame anger, and he took it, wrapped himself tight in the soft cotton, and asked, maybe just to fend off sleep, how far it was to Tobolsk.

A very long way, said Rose.

And then again not, said Ehrenberg. The country was so insanely large that distances lost their meaning. They dissolved into mathematical abstractions.

Something in this answer struck Humboldt as impertinent, but he was too tired to keep thinking about it. It occurred to him that Gauss had spoken of an absolute length, a straight line to which nothing could be added, and which, albeit ultimately, extended so far that every single possible distance was only one section of it. For a matter of seconds, in the limbo between wakefulness and sleep, he had the feeling that this line had something to do with his life, and everything would become bright and clear if only he could grasp what it was. The answer seemed close. He wanted to write to Gauss. But then he fell asleep.

Gauss had calculated that Humboldt still had between three and five years to live. He had recently started to occupy himself with death statistics again. It was a contract from the state insurance bank, well paid and, what was more, not mathematically uninteresting. He had just done some rough calculations on the life expectancies of old acquaintances. If he spent an hour counting the number of people who went past the observatory, he could work out from that how many of them would be in their graves in one year, three years, and ten years. This, he said, was something astrologers could copy!

One must not, replied Weber, underestimate the horoscope; a complete and perfect science would have to incorporate it as well, just as galvanic forces were beginning to be incorporated. Besides which the probability bell curve altered nothing in the simple truth that nobody had any idea when he himself would die; dice always roll for the first time.

Gauss asked him to stop talking nonsense. His wife Minna was sickly, so she would die before he did. Then his mother, then himself. That's what statistics said, and that's how it would happen. He kept staring for a time through the telescope at the mirrored scale over the receiver, but the needle didn't move. Weber didn't reply. The impulses must have got lost in transmission again.

They chatted like this frequently. Weber sat there over in the center of town in the physics department, in front of a second coil with an exactly similar needle. Using inductors they exchanged signals at prearranged times. Gauss had tried something similar years ago with Eugen and the heliotropes, but the boy had never been able to pick up the dyadic alphabet. Weber thought the whole thing was a unique discovery that the professor had only to make public and he would be rich and famous. He was already famous, replied Gauss, and actually quite rich too. The idea was so obvious that he was glad to leave it to the numbskulls.

As there was no further communication from Weber, Gauss stood up, pushed his velvet cap back on his neck, and went for a walk. The sky was covered with translucent clouds and it looked like rain.

How many hours had he waited in front of this receiver for a sign from her? If Johanna was out there, just like Weber, only further away and somewhere else, why didn't she use this opportunity? If the dead allowed themselves to be summoned and then packed off again by girls in nightdresses, why would they spurn this first clear device? Gauss blinked. There was something the matter with his eyes, the firmament seemed to be a tracery of cracks. He felt the first drops of rain. Perhaps the dead no longer spoke because they inhabited a more powerful reality, because all this around him already seemed like a dream and a mere half world, a riddle long since solved, but into whose tangles they would have to step again if they wanted to move and make themselves understood. Some tried. The more intelligent avoided it. He sat down on a rock, rainwater ran down over his head and shoulders. Death would come as a recognition of unreality. Then he would grasp what space and time were, the nature of a line, the essence of a number. Maybe he would also grasp why he always felt himself to be a not-quite-successful invention, the copy of someone much more real, placed by a feeble inventor in a curiously second-class universe. He looked around him. Something that winked was moving in a straight line across the sky, very high up. The street in front of him looked broader, the town wall had disappeared and mirrored glass towers were rising between the houses. Metal capsules were pushing themselves along the streets in antlike columns, the air was filled with a deep rumbling that hung under the sky, and seemed to be rising from the weakly vibrating earth. The wind tasted sour. There was a scorched smell. There was also something invisible he couldn't account for: an electrical vibration detectable only as a faint sick feeling, a wobble in reality itself.

Gauss bent forward, and his movement scattered it all; with a frightened cry he awoke. He was soaked to the skin. He got to his feet and walked quickly back to the observatory. Being old also meant one could nod off to sleep absolutely anywhere.

Humboldt had dozed in so many coaches, had been pulled by so many horses, and had seen so many weed-infested plains that were always the same plain, so many horizons that were always the same horizon, that he no longer felt real even to himself. His companions wore masks against the attacks of the mosquitoes, but they didn't disturb him, they reminded him of his youth and the months he had felt most alive in his entire existence. Their escort had been increased, almost a hundred soldiers rode with them across the taiga at such a tempo that one couldn't begin to think of doing any collecting or measuring. Only once, in the province of Tobolsk, had there been any trouble: in Ischim, Humboldt had fallen into conversation with some Polish convicts, to the displeasure of the police, and then he had slipped away, climbed a hill, and set up his telescope. Minutes later he was surrounded by soldiers. What was he doing there, why was he pointing that barrel thing at the town. His companions had freed him but Rose had dressed him down in front of everyone: he was to stay with the escort, what did he think he was doing?

Their collections grew steadily. Everywhere they were awaited by scientists who gave them their carefully annotated rock and plant samples. A bearded university professor with a bald head and round spectacles presented them with a tiny glass flask containing cosmic ether that he had separated out from the atmosphere with a complicated filtration system. The little flask was so heavy that it needed to be lifted with both hands, and its contents radiated such darkness that even at a short distance things lost their clarity. The substance must be stored with care, said the professor, cleaning the dirty lenses of his glasses, it was extremely flammable. As for him, he'd dismounted the experiment; besides what was in the flask there was nothing left over, and he recommended it be buried deep underground. It was also better not to look at it for too long, it wasn't good for the temper.

More and more of the wooden huts had pagoda roofs, people's eyes were getting narrower, and more and more yurts of the Kyrgyzstani nomads were pitched in the empty landscape. At the border, they were saluted by a regiment of Cossacks, flags fluttering, and a trumpet blared. For a few minutes they journeyed through a boggy no-man's-land, then they were greeted by a Chinese officer. Humboldt gave a speech about evening and morning, Orient and Occident, and universal humanity. Then the Chinese man spoke. There was no interpreter.

He had a brother, said Humboldt quietly to Ehrenberg, who had studied this language too.

The Chinese man raised both hands and smiled. Humboldt presented him with a bale of blue cloth, the Chinese man gave him a roll of parchment. Humboldt opened it, saw that there was writing on it, and stared uneasily at the characters.

But now they must turn back, whispered Ehrenberg, what they were doing was already straining the tsar's goodwill and to actually cross the border was absolutely out of the question.

On the way back they came to a Kalmyk temple. Dark cults flourished here, said Volodin, they really ought to take a look.

A temple servant in a yellow robe and a shaved head led them into the interior. Gold statues smiled, it smelled of burning herbs. A small lama dressed in red and gold was awaiting them. The lama spoke Chinese to the temple servant, and he in turn spoke to Volodin in broken Russian.

He had already heard that a man was on his way who possessed all knowledge.

Humboldt protested: he knew nothing, but he had spent his whole life trying to change this, he had acquired some knowledge and traveled the world, but that was all.

Volodin and the temple servant translated, the lama smiled. He struck his fat stomach with his fist.

Always this here!

Pardon, asked Humboldt.

Here inside, grow big and strong, said the lama.

That was what he had always aimed for, said Humboldt.

The lama touched Humboldt's chest with his soft child's hand. But that was futile. The man who failed to understand that would be restless, would run through the world like a storm, would shatter everything and achieve nothing.

He did not believe in nothing, said Humboldt thickly. He believed in the abundance and the riches of nature.

Nature was unredeemed, said the lama, it breathed despair.

Baffled, Humboldt asked if Volodin had translated correctly.

Dammit, said Volodin, how should he know, the whole thing was meaningless.

The lama asked if Humboldt could wake his dog.

He was sorry, said Humboldt, but he didn't understand this metaphor.

Volodin enquired of the temple servant. Not a metaphor, he then said, the lama's favorite little dog had died the day before yesterday, someone had trodden on it by accident. The lama had retrieved the body and he was asking Humboldt, whom he believed to be a man of great knowledge, to call the animal back.

He couldn't do that, said Humboldt.

Volodin and the temple servant translated, the lama bowed. He knew that an initiate might only do this most rarely but he was begging this favor, the dog was so close to his heart.

He really couldn't do it, said Humboldt, who was slowly becoming dizzy from the smoking herbs. He could rouse no one and nothing from the dead!

He understood, said the lama, what the clever man was telling him with this.

He wasn't telling him anything, cried Humboldt, he simply couldn't do it!

He understood, said the lama, might he at least offer the clever man a cup of tea?

Volodin advised caution, in this area rancid butter got put in tea. If one wasn't used to it, one got really ill.

Humboldt declined with thanks, he couldn't take tea.

He understood this message as well, said the lama.

He wasn't delivering any message, cried Humboldt.

He understood, said the lama.

Uncertainly Humboldt bowed, the lama bowed back, and they were on their way again.

Outside Orenburg another hundred Cossacks arrived to protect them from attacks by the mounted hordes. They were now more than fifty travelers in twelve coaches, with more than two hundred soldiers as escort. They always traveled at top speed and despite Humboldt's requests there were no intermediary halts.

It was too dangerous, said Rose.

It was a long road, said Ehrenberg.

There was much to do, said Volodin.

In Orenburg they were awaited by three Kyrgyzstani sultans who had come with an enormous retinue to meet the man who knew everything. Humboldt asked in a half whisper if he might climb a few hills, he was most interested by the rock formations and it was a long time since he'd measured the air pressure.

Later, said Ehrenberg. Now there would be games!

The evening before they were due to set off again, Humboldt managed to complete some magnetic measurements in the secrecy of his room. Next morning he had back spasms and from then on he walked rather bent over. Rose helped him deferentially into the coach. As they passed a column of prisoners, he forced himself not to look out of the window.

At Astrakhan Humboldt stepped into the first steamship of his life. Two motors sent stinking smoke into the air, the steel body of the boat wallowed out heavily and unwillingly into the water. The foam seemed to glitter faintly in the half-light of dawn. They went ashore on a tiny island. The feet of buried tarantulas stuck up out of the sand. When Humboldt touched them, they twitched, but the creatures didn't run away. Looking almost happy, he made some sketches. He would use them for a long chapter in his travel book.

He didn't really think so, said Rose. He was the one entrusted with doing the descriptions, so Humboldt didn't have to spend time on it.

But he wanted to do it himself, said Humboldt.

He didn't want to be pushing himself forward, said Rose, but he did have his orders from the king.

The ship left its moorings and soon the island was out of sight. They were surrounded by thick fog, water and sky no longer distinguishable from each other. Occasionally a walrus head with its big whiskers surfaced. Humboldt stood in the bow, staring out, and gave almost no reaction when Rose said it was time to go back.

Back where?

First back to land, said Rose, then to Moscow, then Berlin.

So this was the end, said Humboldt, the zenith, the final turn? He would go no further?

Not in this life, said Rose.

It turned out that the ship had gone off course. No one had reckoned with such fog, the captain hadn't brought any charts, and nobody knew which way was terra firma. They sailed around aimlessly, as the fog swallowed all sounds except the thudding of the engines. It was beginning to get dangerous, said the captain, the fuel wouldn't last forever and if they got too far out, not even God would be able to do anything. Volodin and the captain embraced, several of the professors began to drink, and a tearful hilarity took hold.

Rose went to Humboldt in the bow. They needed the assistance of the Great Navigator. Without him they were going to die.

And never go back, asked Humboldt.

Rose nodded.

Simply disappear, sail the Caspian Sea at the apogee of one's life and never come back?

Exactly, said Rose.

Become one with the infinity of space, finally disappear into landscapes one had dreamed of as a child, walk into a picture, walk out the other side, and never go home?

So to speak, said Rose.

That way. Humboldt pointed left, where the gray seemed a little paler, with whitish streaks.

Rose went to the captain and pointed him in the opposite direction. Half an hour later they reached the coast.

In Moscow, there was the biggest ball that they had attended to date. Humboldt appeared in a blue frock coat, was jostled this way and that, and officers saluted him, ladies curtseyed, professors bowed, then it went silent and Officer Glinka read out a poem that began with the burning of Moscow and ended with a verse about Baron Humboldt, the Prometheus of modern times. The applause went on for fifteen minutes. When Humboldt, slightly hoarse and quavering, wanted to give a speech about earth's magnetism, the rector of the university interrupted to present him with a lock of Peter the Great's hair. Talk and chatter, whispered Humboldt in Ehrenberg's ear, no science. He must remember to tell Gauss that he understood much better now.

I know you understand, Gauss replied. You have always understood more, my poor friend, than you know. Minna asked him if he wasn't feeling well. He asked her to leave him in peace, he'd been thinking out loud. He was in an irritable mood, not least because of the smiling Chinaman who had looked at him all night, such behavior was unacceptable even in a dream. Besides which he'd been sent yet another paper on the astral geometry of space, this time from none other than old Martin Bartels. So he's managed to overtake me after all these years, he said, and it seemed as if it wasn't Minna who answered him, but Humboldt in his express coach already racing toward St. Petersburg: things are the way they are and when we recognize them, they are the same as when recognized by others or indeed by no one at all. How do you mean, asked the

285

tsar, who had been about to drape Humboldt with the sash of the Order of St. Anna but stopped in midgesture. Hastily Humboldt assured him that he had only said one should not overestimate the achievements of a scientist, a researcher was not a creator, he didn't invent anything, he didn't conquer lands, he didn't produce bounty, he neither sowed nor did he reap, and he would be followed by others, and still others, who would know more and then even more until finally everything was just swallowed up again. Frowning, the tsar laid the sash over his shoulders, there were cries of Vivat and Bravo, and Humboldt tried very hard to not stand with a bent back. Before, on the great ceremonial staircase he had noticed that some buttons in his dress shirt were open, and he had blushed and been forced to ask Rose to do them up, the latest thing was that his fingers were suddenly so stiff. Now the golden hall swam before his eyes, the chandeliers were shining as if their light were coming from some other source, there was clapping everywhere and a dark-skinned poet with a soft voice read out a poem. Humboldt wished he had told Gauss about the letter that had been waiting for him, crumpled and stained, in St. Petersburg, having taken a year to get there. His days, wrote Bonpland, were heavy and slow, the earth had shrunk until it contained only him, his house, and the land around it, everything beyond that belonged to the invisible world of the president, he was quite calm, he had given up all hope, he expected the worst and had made his peace, so to say; I miss you, old friend. I have never met anyone who liked plants the way you did. Humboldt

286

jumped; Rose had touched his upper arm. Everyone around the large table was looking at him. He got to his feet, but all during his somewhat confused dinner speech he was thinking of Gauss. This Bonpland, the professor would certainly have replied, really did have bad luck, but do we two have anything to complain about? No cannibal ate you, no ignoramus struck me dead. Isn't it slightly shaming how easy it all was for us? And now what's happening is only what always had to happen one day: our Inventor has had enough of us. Gauss laid aside his pipe, pulled his velvet cap over the back of his head, returned the Russian dictionary and the little volume of Pushkin to the shelf, and prepared to go for his preprandial walk. His back hurt, as did his stomach, and there was singing in his ears. But his health really wasn't that bad. Others had died, he was still here. He could still think, admittedly not about very complicated things any more, but enough to deal with the essentials. The treetops swayed above his head, in the distance was the dome of his observatory, later in the night he would go to his telescope and more out of habit than expecting to find anything, he would follow the band of the Milky Way toward the distant spiral nebula. He thought of Humboldt. He would have liked to wish him a good journey back, but in the end one never had a good journey back, every time one was a little weaker and finally one didn't come back at all. Perhaps it really did exist after all, the light-extinguishing ether. But of course it did, thought Humboldt in his coach, he had it with him right here in one of the wagons, he just didn't remember which one any more, there were a hundred packing chests and he'd lost his overview. Suddenly he turned to Ehrenberg. Facts! Ah, said Ehrenberg. Facts, Humboldt repeated, he still had facts, he would write them all down, a vast work full of facts, every fact in the world, contained in a single book, all facts and nothing but facts, the entire cosmos all over again, but stripped of error, fantasy, dream, and fog; facts and numbers, he said in an uncertain voice, they were maybe what could save one. If he thought, for example, that they had been traveling for twenty-three weeks, that they'd covered fourteen thousand five hundred versts, visited six hundred and fifty-eight stopping points, and, he hesitated, used twelve thousand two hundred and twenty-four horses, then the chaos became graspable and one felt better. But as the first suburbs of Berlin flew past and Humboldt imagined Gauss at that very moment staring through his telescope at heavenly bodies, whose paths he could sum up in simple formulas, all of a sudden he could no longer have said which of them had traveled afar and which of them had always stayed at home.

The Tree

As Eugen watched the coastline vanish, he lit up the first pipe of his life. It did not taste good, but apparently one could get used to it. He had a beard now and saw himself for the first time as no longer a child.

The morning following his arrest seemed to be far behind him. The commander of gendarmerie with the big mustaches had stormed into his cell and boxed him twice on the ears with such force that his jaw was put out of joint. Soon afterwards the interrogation began: a remarkably polite man in a morning coat asked him sadly why he'd done it. Resisting arrest had dropped him into the devil's cauldron, had it really been necessary?

But he hadn't resisted, cried Eugen.

The secret policeman asked if he was calling the Prussian police liars.

Eugen begged him to make contact with his father.

Sighing, the secret policeman asked if he really believed they hadn't already done that. He bent forward, took careful hold of Eugen by both ears, and slammed his head down against the tabletop.

When Eugen regained consciousness, he was lying in a bed with clean sheets along the wall of a hospital ward with barred windows. This was not one of the bad places, said an elderly sister, this was only for the aristocracy or people someone had intervened for, he should be happy.

Toward evening the polite secret policeman appeared. Everything had been sorted out, Eugen would leave the country. A journey overseas was in the air.

He wasn't sure, said Eugen, that was an awfully long way away.

It wasn't a recommendation, replied the secret policeman, the idea was not up for discussion, and if Eugen knew the fate he was escaping, he would weep for joy.

In the evening, his father came. He sat down on the edge of the bed and asked how he could have done such a thing to his mother.

He hadn't intended to, said Eugen, weeping, he didn't know about any of it, he didn't want to go away.

Done is done, said his father, patted him absentmindedly on the shoulder, and pushed some money under his pillow. The Baron had arranged everything, he was a fine man, even if somewhat mad.

Eugen asked what he was going to live on.

His father shrugged his shoulders. Had he ever thought about magnetic fields?

Fields?

Functions of the sphere, said his father reflectively. That must be how it was done. He twitched, and looked at Eugen as if he were coming out of a dream.

Whatever, he would manage it! Then he hugged Eugen so tight that his shoulder knocked against Eugen's jaw; for a few seconds he was speechless with pain. When he could think clearly again, his father was gone. Only now did he understand that he would never see him again.

Three days later he reached the port. While waiting for the ferry to England he fell into conversation with three men traveling for business, amiable people, not very intelligent, working for new banking houses, and who invited him to join them in a game of cards. He won. A little at first, then more and more, and eventually so much that they took him for a swindler and he had to leave in a hurry. And all he had done was to use Giordano Bruno's method of taking note of the cards, which his father had taught him years before: one transformed every card in one's head into the figure of a man or an animal, the sillier the better, so that they made up a story. If one practiced, one could keep a game of thirty-two cards in one's head. He'd never succeeded back then, and his father had finally cursed and given up. But now he could do it without difficulty.

In another tavern he drank too much. The air in front of him seemed to flicker and all his limbs felt floppy. The urge to sleep was so powerful that he almost failed to notice the young woman who was suddenly sitting beside him. Not that young, as he realized from up close, and not that pretty either, but when he lied and said he had no money, she asked him, insulted, if he thought she was one of those, and just to show her that he didn't, he took her up with him to his room. On

291

the way he wondered if it was appropriate to tell her that she was his first woman, and he only had the vaguest idea what he was supposed to do. But then it all turned out to be easy, and when he felt her hands on his cheeks in the semidarkness, he was so happy and so tired that he would almost have dropped off to sleep if she hadn't known how to keep him awake, and it no longer mattered how young she was or how she looked, and when it dawned on him next morning that she was gone along with all his winnings, he couldn't find it in himself to be angry. How easy everything was when you left home.

Then he reached England: strange people, a language made up of the oddest sounds, strange place signs, and strange food. Supposedly millions lived in London, but he couldn't imagine it; a million human beings, it made no sense. At the inn where he stayed, a letter reached him from Humboldt, recommending that he take one of the new steamships. He gave advice about how to deal with uncivilized peoples: one must appear to be friendly and interested and must neither conceal one's circumspection nor fail to impart lessons, complacency about the ignorance of others was a form of condescension. Eugen had to laugh. As if he were moving to live among uncivilized peoples! Not one word from his father. At night, he couldn't sleep for loneliness and homesickness. He took the first steamship on which there was an available berth.

There were few passengers aboard, steamships on the ocean passage were a new thing, too new for most people. The sky was low and cloudy, Eugen's pipe went out, he wanted to light it again but the wind was too strong. The captain, who had learned that he understood something of mathematics, invited him onto the bridge.

Was he interested in navigation?

Not in the slightest, said Eugen.

In earlier days, said the captain, such heavy cloud cover would have been a problem, but these days one navigated without the stars, there were exact clocks. Any amateur with a Harrison chronometer could circumnavigate the globe.

So, asked Eugen, was the era of the great navigators over? No more Bligh, no more Humboldt?

The captain thought. Eugen wondered why people always took so long to answer. It wasn't a difficult question! It was over, the captain said finally, and it would never return.

In the night, when Eugen couldn't sleep, more as a result of excitement than the noise of the engines and the snoring of his Irish cabinmate, a real storm blew up: waves pounded against the steel hull with incredible force, the engines howled, and when Eugen tumbled out on deck he was hit by such a blast of spray that he almost fell overboard. He fled back to the cabin dripping wet. The Irishman interrupted his prayers.

He had a large family, he said in poor French, he was responsible for them, he could not die. His father had been hardhearted and incapable of love, his mother had died young, now God was taking him too.

His mother was still alive, said Eugen, and his father had loved a great deal, just not him. And he didn't believe God already wanted his company.

Next morning the ocean was as flat as a lake again. The captain hunched over his charts, murmuring, looked through his sextant, and consulted the Harrison clock. They were way off course, now they would need to take on more fuel.

So they made a stop at Tenerife. The light was dazzlingly bright, a parrot watched them curiously from the balcony of a newly built customhouse. Eugen went ashore. Men were screaming orders, crates were being unloaded, and scantily dressed women were sauntering up and down with tiny steps. A beggar asked for alms, but Eugen had no more money. A cage came open and a horde of shrieking little monkeys exploded away from it in all directions. Eugen left the harbor behind and went toward the outline of the Teide, the big mountain. He wondered what it would be like to be up at the top. One must be able to see very far and the air would be so clear.

There was a monument by the side of the road. A relief showed the mountain, and next to it a man with a top hat, muffler, and morning coat. Eugen couldn't make anything of the inscription except for the name. He sat down on an outcropping of rock, blew little clouds of smoke into the air, and looked at the picture on the stone. A local wearing a poncho and a woolen cap stopped, pointed at it, said something in Spanish, pointed at the ground, then in the air, then at the ground again. A millipede with unusually long feelers climbed Eugen's trouser leg. He looked around. So many new plants. He wondered what they were all called. On the other hand — who cared! They were just names.

He came to a walled garden, with a door that was standing open. Orchids clambered around the trunks of palms, and the twittering of a hundred birds filled the air. A very thick tree grew near the wall, which was clearly of recent construction. Its bark was scarred and raw, and high above the trunk opened out into a bush of branches. Eugen hesitated, then moved into its shade, leaned against the trunk, and closed his eyes. When he opened them again, a man with a rake was standing in front of him and began to curse. Eugen smiled appeasingly. The tree must be very old? The gardener stamped his foot on the ground and pointed to the exit. Eugen asked to be excused, he had been resting, for a moment he had believed he was someone else, or perhaps nobody, it was such a pleasant place. The gardener raised the rake threateningly, and Eugen left in haste.

The steamship cast off early in the morning, and after a few hours the islands were out of sight. For days the ocean was so calm that Eugen had the impression they weren't moving at all. But again and again they overtook sailing ships with full rigging, and twice they passed other steamers. One night Eugen thought he saw a flickering in the distance, but the captain advised him to pay no attention, the sea sent mirages, sometimes it even seemed to dream like a human being.

Then the bigger waves came back, a ragged bird came out of the mist, screamed aggrievedly, and disappeared again. The Irishman asked Eugen if they should join together to start a business, a little company.

Why not, said Eugen.

He also had a sister, said the Irishman, she was unattached, she wasn't a beauty, but she could cook.

Cook, said Eugen, good.

He stuffed his pipe with the last tobacco, went to the bow, and stood there, eyes watering in the wind, until something began to delineate itself in the evening haze, at first transparent and not quite real, but then gradually becoming clearer, and the captain laughed as he replied that no, this time it was no chimera and no summer lightning, it was America.

Also available in ISIS Large Print:

King Henry

Douglas Galbraith

1915. Neutral America is debating the proper response to the war in Europe. Increasingly involved in this debate is Henry Ford. He is against war — it is bad for business.

Ford knows how to make a headline, and when he declares that he will give up all he possesses to stop the build-up to war, the papers get to work. Enter the peace-activist Rosika Schwimmer, who persuades him to send a Peace Ship to Europe, set up a mediation commission and vow to "get the boys out of the trenches by Christmas".

Based on one of the most extraordinary episodes of the early 20th century, this is a strikingly contemporary story of a well-intentioned king with a court that has run mad.

ISBN 978-0-7531-7906-2 (hb)
ISBN 978-0-7531-7907-9 (pb)

A Boy of Good Breeding

Miriam Toews

Life in Winnipeg hasn't worked out so well for Knute and her daughter. But living with her parents back in her hometown of Algren and working for the long-time mayor, Hosea Funk, has its own challenges. Knute finds herself mixed up in Hosea's attempts to achieve his dream of meeting the Prime Minister — even though that means keeping the town's population at an even 1500. It's not an easy task, with citizens threatening to move back, and one Algrenian on the verge of giving birth to twins — or possibly triplets.

Full of humour and larger-than-life characters, A Boy of Good Breeding is a warm-hearted novel about families that have been split up but are inexorably drawn back together.

ISBN 978-0-7531-7860-7 (hb)
ISBN 978-0-7531-7861-4 (pb)

The Fall of Troy

Peter Ackroyd

Sophia Chrysanthis is only 16 when the German archaeologist Herr Obermann comes wooing: he wants a Greek bride who knows her Homer. Sophia passes his test, and soon she is tying canvas sacking to her legs so that she can kneel in the trench, removing the earth methodically, lifting out amphorae and bronze vessels without damaging them.

The atmosphere at Troy is tense and mysterious. Sophia finds herself increasingly baffled by the past . . . not only the remote past that Obermann is so keen to share with her in the form of his beloved epics of the Trojan wars, but also his own, recent past — a past that he has chosen to hide from her.

But she, too, is very good at the art of archaeology . . .

ISBN 978-0-7531-7804-1 (hb)
ISBN 978-0-7531-7805-8 (pb)

Dream Angus

Alexander McCall Smith

If he's in the right mood, divine Angus might grant you sight of your true love in a dream; you might even fall in love with him — but he'll never love you back. He's too busy making mischief — stealing the palace of the gods from his father, turning his enemies into pigs etc — until he is trapped by his own romantic games and falls for an unattainable woman, doomed to seek her forever.

In 20th century Scotland, Angus's troubled alter ego searches for his true family; a psychotherapist who helps people understand their dreams, his life seems to parallel that of his mythic namesake, until we ask — could they be the one and the same?

Mesmerically weaving together the tales of the Celtic god and the Scottish scientist, Alexander McCall Smith unites dream and reality, leaving us to wonder: what is life, but the pursuit of our dreams?

ISBN 978-0-7531-7718-1 (hb)
ISBN 978-0-7531-7719-8 (pb)